Every Girl's Handbook

Hamlyn

London · New York · Sydney · Toronto

New Revised edition 1978
Second impression 1979

Published by
THE HAMLYN PUBLISHING GROUP LIMITED
London · New York · Sydney · Toronto
Astronaut House, Feltham, Middlesex, England

ISBN 0 600 33162 8
Printed in Italy

CONTENTS

HEALTH AND HYGIENE

HOME MAKING

HANDICRAFTS

HOBBIES

NATURAL HISTORY

OUTDOOR ACTIVITIES

THE WORLD OF SPORT

FIFTY FAMOUS WOMEN IN HISTORY

THE WORLD – USEFUL FACTS AND FIGURES

PEOPLE AND THE NEW WORLD

PEOPLE AND SCIENCE

PEOPLE AND LANGUAGE

HEALTH AND HYGIENE

Looking After Yourself

This chapter is designed to help you to learn how to look after yourself. There are lots of tips that should help you to be vital, relaxed, confident and good to look at.

If you are healthy and relaxed you can tackle anything that comes your way. If you look good, there is nothing that will give you more confidence. All these benefits come from knowing how to look after your body, so learn all you can about health, hygiene and good grooming – the first steps to basic beauty.

Health Foods

Yoghourts, both plain and fruit, are full of vitamins A and D, marvellous for skin and hair. Bread is also good for you, so if you need to fill up a little, eat a couple of slices of wholemeal bread a day, which provides extra protein, iron and calcium, B vitamins and roughage. Calcium for teeth, nails and bones is contained in milk, cream and cheese. Try to consume a pint a day. Fresh fruit and vegetables are essential. Citrus fruits are a good source of vitamin C, essential for good skin. Since the body cannot retain or store this vitamin, you should have a daily intake of either an orange or grapefruit. Liver is rich in iron, so good for your blood, so try to eat this once every week. Eat green vegetables for vitamin B which is also contained in egg yolk and other dairy products. Eat proteins, contained in meat, fish, eggs and cheese for body building and energy. Take a restricted amount of sugar for energy and warmth and cut out all the unhealthy starchy foods like cakes, biscuits, potatoes.

Every Girl's Guide to Healthy Eating

You are what you eat! If you want to be vital, energetic, have super-soft skin, sparkling eyes, a glowing head of hair and good teeth and nails – diet is the way to achieve them. Of course, the obvious reaction to diet is that it can help you to loose weight, which is another all important health factor, too. Add a trim figure to the list and you have all the reasons for eating a sensible, healthy, well balanced diet.

As a rule all the non-nutritious foods give the problems. Sweet and starchy foods make you overweight, give you a spotty skin and ruin your teeth. Try to re-educate your eating habits, fill up on proteins and fresh fruit and vegetables. Easier said than done? Allow yourself the odd treat to avoid getting miserable and giving up altogether. If you want to loose weight, do so only with the permission of your doctor and use our calorie chart to help you add up your daily intake. A limit of 1,200–1,300 calories per day is correct for the average girl to loose weight.

Meats

Bacon	– lean	2 oz	175
Bacon	– fat	2 oz	260
Beef	– lean	4 oz	210
Beef	– fat	4 oz	300
Ham	– lean	4 oz	265
Ham	– fat	4 oz	375
Kidneys		4 oz	145
Lamb	– lean	4 oz	230
Lamb	– fat	4 oz	375
Liver	–	4 oz	160
Pork	– lean	4 oz	270
Pork	– fat	4 oz	450
Sausages:			
Beef	–	2 oz	120
Pork	–	2 oz	145
Veal and Ham Pie		4 oz	300

Cheese and Eggs

Cheddar cheese	1 oz	120
Cottage cheese	1 oz	40/50
Cream cheese	1 oz	145
Dutch cheese	1 oz	90
Processed cheese	1 oz	120
Eggs (boiled or poached) 1 egg	2 oz	80
Egg (fried or scrambled)	2 oz	130

Fish

Cod fillets	4 oz	95
Haddock	4 oz	120
Hake	4 oz	90
Herring (one)	4 oz	190
Mackerel	4 oz	90
Plaice	4 oz	90

Salmon (tinned)	4 oz	190
Sardines	2 oz	160
Shrimps	4 oz	55

Poultry

Chicken	4 oz	165
Duck	4 oz	190
Goose	4 oz	355
Turkey	4 oz	185

Milk and Fats

Butter	$\frac{1}{4}$ oz	65
Lard	$\frac{1}{4}$ oz	60
Margarine	$\frac{1}{4}$ oz	55
Cream, single	1 oz	55
Cream, double	1 oz	100
Milk, whole	$\frac{1}{2}$ pt	175
Milk, skimmed	$\frac{1}{2}$ pt	70
Milk, condensed	1 oz	100
Milk, evaporated	1 oz	45
Yoghourt	$\frac{1}{4}$ pt	100

Biscuits, Cakes and Sweets

Biscuits, plain	1 oz	110
Biscuits, sweet	1 oz	140
Cake, plain	2 oz	150
Cake, rich	2 oz	210
Doughnut	2 oz	195
Boiled sweets	1 oz	120
Chocolate, plain or milk	1 oz	150
Syrup	1 oz	180
Sugar, white	$\frac{1}{2}$ oz	55
Sugar, brown	$\frac{1}{2}$ oz	50
Honey	1 oz	80
Ice-cream	2 oz	115
Jams and jellies	$\frac{1}{2}$ oz	35/60

Nuts

Almond	1 oz	170
Brazil	1 oz	90
Chestnuts	2 oz	75
Peanuts	2 oz	335
Walnuts	1 oz	185

Breads and Cereals

Bread, brown or white	1 oz	70
Starch reduced roll	1 roll	18
Starch reduced crispbread	1 oz	110/120
Cornflower or Custard powder	1 oz	100
Cornflakes and most cereals	1 oz	110
Spaghetti and Macaroni, dry	1 oz	80/100
Rice, dry	1 oz	90

Beverages

Cider	$\frac{1}{2}$ pt	120
Chocolate	1 cup	180
Cocoa (half milk)	1 cup	110
Coffee, black	1 cup	0
Coffee, milk and sugar	1 cup	85
Fruit squash diluted	1 glass	100
Malted drinks	1 cup	205
Mineral waters	1 glass	100
Tea with milk	1 cup	20
Tea with milk and sugar	1 cup	75
Beers, according to strength	$\frac{1}{2}$ pt	130/210

Wine, dry	1 glass	70
Wine, sweet	1 glass	90

Fruit

Apple, raw	4 oz	45
Apple, cooked	4 oz	75
Apricots, fresh	4 oz	30
Apricots, canned	4 oz	60
Apricots, dried	4 oz	200
Banana, medium		80/100
Blackberries, fresh	4 oz	30
Blackberries canned	4 oz	75
Cherries, fresh	4 oz	45
Cherries, canned	4 oz	95
Coconut, fresh	1 oz	170
Coconut, desiccated	1 oz	180
Dates, dried	1 oz	85
Figs, dried	2 oz	115
Gooseberries	4 oz	40
Grapefruit	4 oz	25
Grapes	4 oz	60
Lemon	3 oz	30
Melon	4 oz	16
Orange	6 oz	40
Peaches, fresh	4 oz	30
Peaches, canned	4 oz	64
Pear, fresh	6 oz	50
Pear, canned	6 oz	75
Pineapple, fresh	6 oz	65
Pineapple, canned	6 oz	120
Plums, fresh	4 oz	30
Plums, canned	4 oz	80
Raisins	2 oz	125

Raspberries, fresh	4 oz	25
Rhubarb, fresh	4 oz	5
Strawberries	4 oz	30
Tangerine	3 oz	20

Vegetables

Asparagus	3 oz	15
Beans, baked	4 oz	100
Beans, broad	4 oz	60
Beans, french or runner	4 oz	15
Beetroot	2 oz	15
Brussels sprouts	4 oz	20
Cabbage	4 oz	20
Carrots	2 oz	15
Cauliflower	4 oz	20
Celery	2 oz	5
Cucumber	2 oz	10
Leeks	4 oz	15
Lettuce	2 oz	10
Marrow	4 oz	10
Mushrooms	2 oz	2
Onions	4 oz	25
Parsley	$\frac{1}{4}$ oz	0
Parsnips	4 oz	55
Peas, fresh	4 oz	75
Potatoes, boiled two medium		95
Potatoes, fried two medium		270
Radishes	1 oz	2
Spinach	4 oz	20
Tomatoes, fresh	4 oz	20
Turnips	4 oz	40

13

Spot-reducing Exercises

One or two chosen exercises performed regularly night and morning will give definite results. Work up from six repeats to a maximum of fifteen. A trim, well-proportioned figure is one of the first steps to beauty.

Hips 1. Sit on floor, clasp arms round knees then rock from side to side and backwards and forwards. 2. Lie with legs about a foot off the ground. Count to ten, then slowly lower them to the ground. 3. Stand with feet apart. Jump in the air and, as you do so, throw arms above head and turn toes in. Jump again bringing arms down and turning feet out again. Both exercises 2 and 3 are good for thighs, too.

Tummy 1. Lie with your feet under a firm piece of furniture such as a bed or chest of drawers. Clasp your hands behind your head and rise slowly to a sitting position while breathing in. Slowly lie down again, breathing out. 2. Try back-bends. Stand a little away from a wall or door. Throw your arms above your head whilst breathing in and bend backwards to touch the wall. Return to upright position. Increase the distance as you get used to the exercise.

Waist and Midriff 1. Reach for the sky, with hands climbing until you are stretched to your limit. Relax with hands by your side. 2. Stand, feet slightly apart, with arms outstretched at sides. Moving the upper part of the body only, turn as far as you can to the left, return to centre, then repeat movement to the right.

Legs 1. Holding back of chair swing each leg in turn as high as it will go both backwards and forwards, keeping toe pointed. 2. Lie flat on floor, raise up onto shoulders with hips supported on hands and elbows on the ground. Do cycling in the air for 3–4 minutes then do scissor movement – swinging legs wide apart, then crossing them.

Bust 1. Lie flat on floor with hands clasped behind your head. Bring elbows forward so that they touch, or nearly touch, then slowly let them back to the floor. 2. Sit cross-legged and circle

14

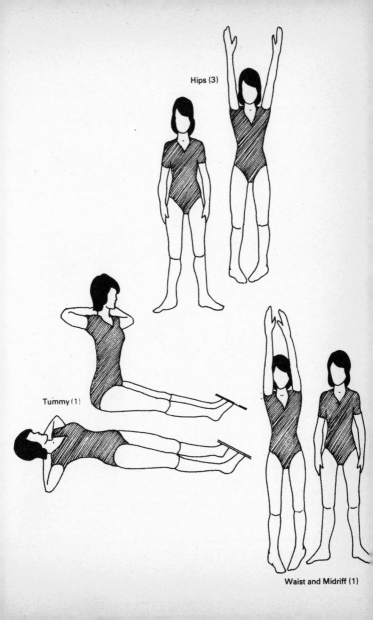

Hips (3)

Tummy (1)

Waist and Midriff (1)

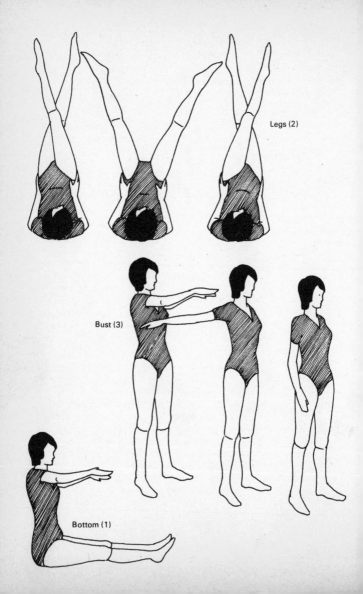

Legs (2)

Bust (3)

Bottom (1)

arms like a windmill. 3. Stand, feet slightly apart, arms stretched straight in front of you, then fling arms vigorously out and backwards. Continuing the movement swing arms forward again, crossing hands before repeating the exercise.

Bottom 1. Sit upright with legs straight out in front of you. Raise arms to shoulder level, then inch yourself forward by walking on your buttocks ten paces forwards, then ten paces back.

Bathtime

Healthy hygiene, good grooming and basic beauty all begin in the bathroom. You can make bathnight fun, not a chore, and you are certain to feel fresh and glowing as a result. A bathnight routine is something you can enjoy and if you follow our tips, will become a well-founded habit that you can always keep to.

Ideally you should have a shower or bath daily, or at least a very thorough wash. Personal freshness is essential for everyone. Perspiration smell is caused by the bacteria on the skin attacking the sweat when it reaches the surface of the skin. Perspiration odour doesn't start until about the age of ten when the special Apocrine glands develop. They are found mainly under the arms and between the legs.

Once a week take time to have a lazy bathnight and catch up on all the little chores you would otherwise forget to do. First of all run your bath and add some bubble bath if it is available. Alternatively you can soften the water with a large spoon of borax or powdered water softener. If you are not washing your hair after your bath protect with a shower cap as the steam will make curly hair more frizzy or take the set out of straighter hair. Make sure you have everything you need to hand – soap, nail and back brush, pumice stone and talcum powder. While you are in the bath make an effort to get your circulation going by rubbing a bath brush or loofah briskly all over your arms, legs and especially your back, which is inclined to get oily or spotty between the shoulder blades. Your skin will tingle and the scrubbing should encourage blemishes to disappear. Scrub feet thoroughly and follow the foot care routine on opposite page. The hot steam of the bath will help to open the skin pores on your face. If you suffer from blackheads you should be able to press them out gently with your fingertips and remove with a clean tissue. While you are relaxing in the bath, now is the time to apply a face mask – something you can do occasionally rather than every week. You can find a selection of recipes for making your own face packs on page 23. If you are not doing a face mask wash oily skins gently with soap, water and a complexion brush, or spread moisturiser on dry skins and let the steam help it to sink into the pores. Don't forget to wash in and around your ears carefully (easily forgotten) and last of all body hair can be dealt with. If you are blond or do not have very much hair on your legs, the best advice is never to start shaving at all. From the moment you first shave your legs, the hairs will grow stronger and you will be left with a permanent chore and a rough, stubbly regrow of hair that is particularly irritating and unattractive. So, only undertake this if you have a heavy growth of dark hair that you cannot bear to live with. Underarm hair should be removed since this harbours sweat and perspiration odour – be careful and use an old-fashioned man's hand razor or a special battery-driven ladies' shaver.

After your bath, dry yourself thoroughly and dust all over with talc. After a bath your nails are softened and just right for you to do a manicure and pedicure. Read 'Best Foot Forward' for pedicure routine and 'Pretty Hands' for the manicure tips (pages 20–22). Do this while you are under the hair dryer. Finally, clean your teeth to complete the new, fresh you. 'Sweet Smiles' clearly explains how to clean teeth properly and why it is so important for you to look after your teeth as an investment for the future.

Best Foot Forward

Feet need attention. They do a lot of hard work for you, so

don't ignore them and with comfortable feet your smile may well be brighter, too.

Feet are covered in sweat glands so obviously they need thorough washing. Scrub them when you are in the bath and use a nail brush or pumice stone to remove any dry or flaky skin. Always dry carefully between each toe and dust well afterwards with talc. Thorough drying avoids the possibility of suffering from athletes foot. You can puff talc into shoes, socks and stockings too, to stop them getting hot and sweaty. If you happen to use body lotion after a bath, your feet need nourishment just as much, if not more, than other areas of skin. Always clip your toe nails after the bath, when they are softer. Using toe nail clippers or a rough emery board work your toe nails into a squared shape – which helps prevent the painful problem of ingrowing toe nails. You can feed nails with baby lotion or body lotion. Allow to soak in for a few minutes then wipe off excess with cotton wool.

Footnotes about shoes: The golden rule, never to be broken, is to wear the correct size shoes – in width as well as length. Properly fitting shoes need not be fuddy-duddy these days, so – make sure you are comfortable, avoid heels that are too high and ensure that winter boots allow for thick socks if you intend to wear them inside. Boots that are too tight lead the way to chilblains.

Cold feet – don't suffer, knit yourself a pair of jazzy bed socks!

Sweet Smiles

Knowing how to look after your teeth is extremely important. Without the correct care and diet you could be sporting false teeth at a very early age, so start right now if you haven't been bothering too much before. First of all, diet – the main offender in tooth decay is SUGAR. We all know sweets are bad, but it is not just sweets that do the damage. It is all sugar taken in your diet in any shape or form. Jams, jellies, lollypops, syrup, cakes, biscuits, squashes and chocolate must be limited as well.

You must learn how to clean your teeth properly. Accept that this may take longer than you are used to, and try to be thorough. Brush from the gum to the biting edge, working the bristles between the teeth to dislodge food particles. Don't skimp on the gums, massage them in the same stroke as brushing your teeth and give them an occasional extra massage, rubbing them gently in a circular movement with a little toothpaste on your finger. Brush your teeth in this way, working systematically around the front of the teeth and then on the inside, followed by a sawing movement across the tops of the teeth. If you have any difficulty dislodging particles of food from between teeth, try stretching a length of dental floss down between the teeth and lift, using a sawing movement. This or wooden toothpicks can do the trick.

Brush your teeth after every meal if possible. If not, then just night and morning, remembering to give them a special clean up straight away, if you do indulge in eating half a pound of toffees in one go. If teeth are properly cleaned this prevents plaque forming around the gum edges of the teeth. Plaque forms very easily after food is eaten and bacteria form quickly and thrive in it and start the decay of the enamel and encourage inflamation of the gum. Gum diseases are just as destructive as tooth decay itself. As a rule always use a toothpaste containing fluoride which is a proven force in fighting tooth decay.

Pretty Hands

Learning the art of caring for your hands and doing a professional manicure is time well spent. You don't have to be sporting blood-red nails, or any other extraordinary fashion colour of the moment! Well manicured nails look great without nail polish or with just a hint of a sheen from a natural polish.
1. Remove nail polish.
2. Shape nail, preferably with an emery board. File from each side of the nail towards the centre.

20

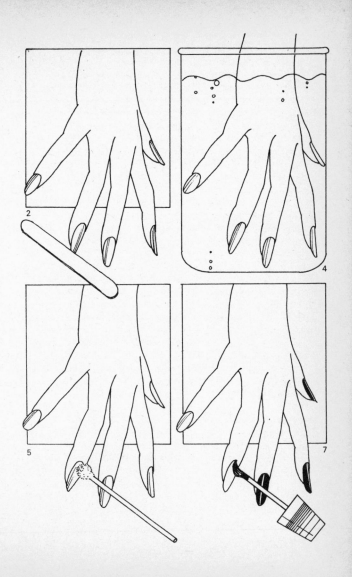

3. Massage cuticles with cuticle remover cream and leave for ten minutes.

4. Soak fingers in warm, soapy water for a few minutes then rinse and dry.

5. Use the blunt end of a cuticle stick (or orange stick) to lift the cuticle, and to clean under tips of nails.

6. Massage hands with handcream, then remove any excess from nails with polish remover.

7. Apply polish. You can use two coats of polish or a special base coat, followed by the coloured polish with a final coat of transparent sealer to minimise chipping. Use three strokes only – centre, then two sides. Do the thumb nail first, then the little finger and work back to the index finger.

8. After each coat, to clean up any excess nail polish, put a wisp of cotton wool around the end of an orange stick, dip in remover and carefully apply to cuticle and finger areas. Do not dab the nail as you will have to start the polish procedure all over again.

9. Make sure you allow enough drying time between coats. Try resting elbows on the table, relax wrists and exercise fingers.

If your nails break or split easily treat them with respect and protect them if you are doing any hard jobs. Also, look to your diet. Build up your nails with high protein food, so eat a lot of meat, fish, cheese, eggs and milk. You can also feed nails by massaging in a drop of nail cream at the base of the nail. If you are a nail biter, concentrate on tidying your nails, put polish on as a deterrent and try to enjoy the prospect of pretty hands. It won't take long, once you have broken the habit, to have truly elegant hands!

Budget Beauty

Natural products often make the best beauty products. They are usually expensive to buy and young skins should not be laden with heavy cosmetics. So try concocting your own products at home and give your skin the occasional treat. Choose one evening a week to have a lazy bath, do your hair, cleanse and tone your skin and then, best of all, follow by an early night and get a full night's sleep.

Skin Tonic Cucumber makes an excellent skin freshener. Rub thin slices over your face and neck. Melon, too has a similar refreshing benefit for the skin. Make up a liquid tonic by saving orange, lemon and grapefruit peels. Score with a knife to get out as much of the natural oils as possible then soak in a pint of cooled boiled water for twenty-four hours. Strain, add juice of lemon or orange and use on cotton wool to freshen skin after washing or cleansing with cream. Another equally good skin tonic can be made with equal quantities of witch hazel and rosewater, both of which you can easily buy from chemists.

Face Masks For normal and oily skins, mix the white of an egg and the juice of a lemon in a saucer. Add enough Fuller's Earth (cheap to buy from chemists) to mix to a stiff paste. Clean your face thoroughly before spreading the mixture on your face. Leave on for fifteen minutes then rinse off with cotton wool and warm water. Dry skins need a nourishing pack. Mix an egg yolk with one tablespoon of powdered skimmed milk or oatmeal and one tablespoon of fresh milk and mix to a cream. Add half a teaspoon of honey and beat in thoroughly. Again, relax for ten to fifteen minutes then gently wash off with warm water.

Hair Conditioners Try massaging a whipped up egg yolk into damp hair after shampooing, then rinse off with tepid water. Use two yolks for long hair. Oil conditioner can be made from olive, almond, castor, coconut or any vegetable oils that may happen to be in the kitchen. Pour the oil into a cup or bottle and stand in a saucepan of hot water for a few minutes. It needs to be warmed, not hot. Apply the warmed oil to partings all over scalp, using a medicine dropper if possible. Put on a well-fitting plastic shower hat to keep in the warmth then wrap a turban on top, using a towel wrung out in hot water. Wait for thirty minutes before shampooing hair. This treatment will do wonders for dry, brittle hair.

Hair Care

Cutting Regular cutting by a professional hairdresser is all important. A good cut is the basis of any hairstyle, however simple, and removes damaged hair and split ends so that your hairstyle will fall into place with the minimum of fuss and trouble.

Washing There is a wide variety of shampoos available, so assess your hair type and use a shampoo that should suit you. You may have to try a few before you find the ideal shampoo for your hair. If you have greasy hair use lemon or medicated shampoos and try hard to resist the temptation to wash your hair too often. Frequent washing and massaging of the scalp encourages the sebum glands to produce more oil than is necessary, thereby increasing your problem. Dry hair can be coped with more easily by the use of conditioning shampoos or a creamy conditioner applied after the shampoo. Dandruff should be treated with the regular use of medicated shampoos.

Drying Never sit and frizzle your hair within close range of an electric fire. If you have a simple, loose style use a hairdryer with a brush attachment and you can brush your hair into a style and dry it all in one process. If it is a hot summer's day and there is no chance of catching a cold, both very curly and straight hair can be left to dry naturally. If you have to set your hair on rollers, dry with a hand dryer or under a hood and make sure hair is absolutely dry before removing rollers or the style will flop instantly and you will lose the benefit of all your efforts.

Brushing Dry and normal hair require daily brushing to stimulate the scalp and distribute the natural sebum evenly, which gives the hair its healthy gloss. Don't overbrush oily hair as the sebum glands do not need extra stimulation. Brushing also removes surface dust and dirt. A certain amount of hair loss is natural and healthy since old hairs make way for new at a rate of 20–100 hairs per day.

Setting If you do have to set your hair, a setting lotion will help the style to last. Towel hair dry after shampooing then comb setting lotion through each section of hair before winding onto rollers. When using rollers be sure to use the correct size for your style and type of hair. Don't wind too much hair onto one roller. Hold each section of hair up at right angles to the scalp and wind down, not backwards. Try not to wind rollers too tightly as this can break hair at the scalp. If hair dries as you are doing your set, re-dampen each section of hair with water.

Hair Appliances There are lots of electrical aids available to help keep your hair under control.

Always be sure to check that any electrical appliance is in perfect order before use. No bare wires should be showing, the plugs should be firmly fixed and remember to be extra careful since you may have wet hands as well as wet hair.

Electric Rollers are excellent if used in limitation. They work best on newly washed damp-dry hair and give a tight and lasting set in about ten minutes. They can also be used on dry hair as a mid-week boost to regain lost bounce and curl. The main caution is not to over-use them. They can make hair dry and brittle and even damage the hair if used excessively. *Curling Tongs* are extra quick and easy to use. Be careful how you handle tongs until you are used to them as it is easy to dab tongs against the face – watch fingers, too. Once you have acquired the knack they are a real aid – they can just help hair to flick under or up (thereby controlling an unruly mop) or they can produce tight curls and even ringlets – according to how much hair you are attempting to curl in one go. Some tongs use steam to make the curls stronger and some have extra attachments. *Hair Dryers* come with a wide range of attachments so that they can do drying and styling in one process. Brush and comb accessories fit to the end of the hot air hose and make blow-drying all the easier. There are compact dryers (without attachments) that can be easily packed and used if travelling. *Hair Straighteners*. There is an appliance which provides a heated comb with which you can straighten out unwanted curls and kinks.

Brushes and Combs. It is important to keep these clean. Give them a thorough wash once a week. Make a routine of doing this when you wash your hair.

How to Live with your Hair If you go *swimming* a lot and prefer not to wear a cap run a little conditioning cream through your hair before you plunge in. Rinse hair thoroughly in fresh water afterwards to remove chlorine (or salty sea water, should you be swimming in the sea). If you don't mind wearing a cap you can twist hair into flat curls and pin. Your hair style may be flattened, but it will be ready to brush into your style after swimming. *Long hair* can be a problem if you like to keep it off your face in hot weather or just for convenience. Try not to use elastic bands as they tear and damage the hair. Instead, use round elastic with bobbles at each end that you can thread one over the other. This is far kinder to your hair and looks pretty too. *Summer sun* can also have a damaging effect on hair. The sun and sea can strip hair of its natural oils, so protect with a hat or scarf whenever possible and re-vitalise hair with protein conditioner. *Curly hair* – if you are tired of curls and long for straighter hair you can always try using the crepe bandage technique. With hair very wet, make a parting and hold one end of the bandage against your head with one hand and wind it round until all your hair is covered except the crown. On drying the bandage shrinks and tightens, holding the hair flat. Now set on large rollers and your natural curls will provide your new style with bounce, not frizz. *Growing out an old style* can be a very tedious business. In the in-between stages when your patience runs out, resort to the hairdresser. Even if you are growing your hair it needs to be reshaped from time to time to keep its shape. Half grown-out fringes can be pinned back with a pretty clip or brush back and hold off face with a scarf folded over into a headband and tied at nape of neck. *Tired of straight hair?* Perms are available in all strengths – you can choose loose curls to give hair bounce or go for tight curls. Home perms are excellent these days and a lot cheaper than the professional versions, providing you have someone who can

26

help you. A light perm is often the answer to living with lank, thin hair that looks nothing worn straight.

Skin Care

Few girls are lucky enough to have a beautiful, normal, trouble-free skin. And, even if you are one of the lucky ones, you should still know how to cleanse and nourish your skin. Routine care is the answer to dealing with any problems, as well as maintaining a good complexion. Always apply creams and lotions with gentle, upward movements to tone the muscles and stimulate the circulation. Downward movements will drag the skin and stretch the muscles. First, you must assess your skin type – for example it is wrong to make the assumption that you have an oily skin just because you suffer from spots because this is not necessarily true at all. Diet can have a drastic effect on the skin, so refer back to first page of this chapter for the foods you should and should not be eating.

Dry Skin will feel tight and stretched across the cheekbones if you wash your face with soap and water. Avoid soap and water and take care with your cleansing routine. Use a light cream or cleansing milk which will penetrate the skin easily and tone with a skin lotion (not astringent). Protect against strong sun and wind with a light moisturiser.

Oily Skin is usually thicker and coarser and large skin pores can easily be seen through a magnifying mirror. This is another type of skin that needs a lot of attention, to prevent the skin from getting clogged up and thereby producing spots and blackheads. Oily skin will benefit from stimulating the circulation. Buy yourself a complexion brush and cleanse by giving the face a thorough brush with warm water and a mildly medicated soap every night. Afterwards apply an astringent and splash with cold water, to help close the pores. A facial sauna once a week will help to draw out the dirt and impurities. Fill a bowl with very hot water and add either the juice of a lemon or a sprinkle of herbs. Protect hair with a bath hat and sit with a large towel over your head. Steam the skin for up to five minutes, then cleanse again to remove the deep-seated dirt. An oily skin can take a face mask more often than others and can be done once a week to help close the pores.

Combination Skin is a mixture of oily and dry skins with the oily patch usually occupying the centre panel of the face – centre forehead, nose, mouth and chin. Use a light cleansing milk all over the face but tone with an astringent down the centre panel. Weaken the astringent by adding water to the cotton wool for toning the rest of the face. Apply a moisturiser to the dryer areas.

Spotty Skin – most girls suffer from the odd spot now and then but acne, a permanently spotty condition of the skin, is suffered by over one and a half million girls in their teens and early twenties. It is usually caused by hormone changes and the stresses of growing up and most girls will eventually grow out of it.

Get your circulation going – try taking up a sport, eat the right foods, ensure that you get enough sleep and take large doses of fresh air. Keep your face thoroughly clean – never let oil and dirt stay long enough to clog the pores. Throw away your flannel. Cleanse as for oily skins and try some of the various medicated creams and lotions available on the market. There are creams that can be applied only to the spots which have a drying, astringent effect and help the spots to peel.

Sensitive Skin is usually extra dry skin, although it can belong to almost any skin type. Sensitive skins tend towards blotchiness, broken veins and rashes. Use only the purest, non-perfumed cosmetics. Never use astringent – only the mildest of toners applied to the face on damp cotton wool. Cleanse, tone and use a mild skin cream at night, being careful to wipe away any surplus that might clog the skin.

Freckles can be very attractive but if you want to temporarily fade them apply neat lemon juice. They will come back as soon as you go into the sun because freckles are patches of pigment which is the skin's protection against sunlight.

28

HOMEMAKING

Room Decor

Your own room is a very important place – the only room in your home where you can be yourself, either to relax or work in. Even if you share with a sister, the room can be cleverly planned to suit both your needs. Above all, your room should express your personality, carry your own special style by your choice of colour scheme, bedroom accessories and wall decorations. It can be great fun to transform your room and the cost need not be great since you can make most knick-knacks for yourself out of odds and ends. You just need imagination and patience. So, if your bedroom needs improving, see if any of our tips and ideas appeal to you.

Basic room planning There are various important points you should consider carefully before you finalise your scheme. For example, is the room small, dark, have a high or low ceiling or rather too many obstructions to wall space, such as fireplace, airing cupboard or meter cupboard? Or perhaps there is a dormer window and sloping roof. All these factors will determine colour schemes, arrangement of storage space and best use of natural lighting.

A small, dark room needs to be given a feeling of light and space. Keep to light colours, or preferably white, and use bright colours for your accessories. If possible try to arrange all your storage items along one wall (which can be an attractive feature in itself), leaving the rest of the room free as uncluttered living space. For example a chest of drawers can stand next to wardrobe or hanging space. The top of the chest can be used as a dressing table and the space above can be utilised by bracketing bookshelves or a mirror to the wall. A large extra shelf above the wardrobe can accommodate suitcases and other bulky items not in constant use.

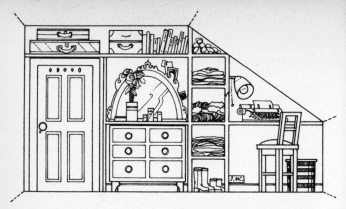

A room with a dormer window and sloping roof
is one that needs careful planning. Standing room is the problem. Place the head of the bed where the roof is at its lowest –
leaving enough room to sit and plenty of room to lie down!
Place any working space such as desk or chest under the window,
which again allows plenty of space for sitting and is conveniently placed near natural lighting. Dormer windows are usually
rather small, so conserve light by using a roller blind instead of
curtains. Place your wardrobe where the ceiling is at its highest.
If the room is dark a large wall mirror will help reflect light. To
make the most of the unusual shapes in the room go for a fairly
strong colour on the walls and contrast with a light ceiling.
Sharing a room with bunk beds can be made more fun
by arranging the room at two height levels. Bunk beds are an
obvious space saver, so an arrangement of high shelves which
can be reached from the top bunk makes life more pleasant for
the top sleeper with a chance to have her own things around
her. The relevant wall space can belong to each bunk occupier,
so that there should be no problem about who puts what on
the wall. The rest of the room has to be shared and could take
on a definite colour scheme to prevent the room from looking
bitty – try to match bedspreads, curtains and perhaps use the
same material to cover an old storage chest. Scatter cushions
can be placed on top to make extra seating.

Bedroom accessories. Here are some ideas for easy to-make accessories. If you have changed the colour scheme and arrangement of your room a few pretty accessories will give the final finishing touches.

A pretty wastepaper bin can easily be made from a large round tin, painted inside and the outside covered with a self-adhesive fablon or hessian if you prefer a more textured look. Be sure to use a fabric adhesive if using hessian and stick a braid trimming around the top and bottom of the bin when the hessian has dried out.

A flower vase can be made using the same principle as the wastepaper bin. Choose a small tin or a taller one, cover and place a small glass jar inside to hold the water for fresh flowers. If you have a dried flower or paper flower arrangement put a closely-fitting round of 'oasis' in the base of the vase which will hold the stems or wires permanently in position.

Two lampshades to make Covering a lampshade frame with fabric is more difficult than it looks unless you use the popular bell-shaped frame. For this, measure the diameter of the frame at the widest point, then allow 3–4 cms for the seam and sew to form a tube. Cut the fabric 13–15 cms longer than the frame and use this allowance to turn under a hem, top and bottom, through which you thread elastic. The elastic should be pulled tightly at the top to fit the frame and looser at the bottom so that you can stretch the cover over the frame at its widest point. Now make a narrow frill or use a fringed braid and neatly slip stitch to the bottom fabric cover at the widest point. A lampshade with a difference can be made by using a simple cylinder-shape frame. Cut out circles of silver foil using a cardboard template 4 cms in diameter. Take care not to crumple the foil. Brush one side of each circle with glue and lay them, glued side up, half a centimetre apart on a piece of newspaper. Lay thread (preferably silver) down the centre of enough circles to fit the depth of your frame and cover with a second foil circle, pressing down well to stick them together. When you have enough strings tie them carefully to the top and bottom of the frame. To finish stitch a pretty braid around the top and bottom of the frame.

A bits and pieces board A useful item to hang on a bedroom wall. Pin anything to it that appeals to you – pictures, photographs, cartoons and personal reminders. You can even pin items of jewellery that would otherwise get tangled in a jewellery box such as long strings of beads. Use a piece of chipboard as a base – 1 metre square would be a reasonable size, and cover with a sheet of bright coloured felt the same size. Carefully stick the felt down with a clear adhesive and finish by trimming the edges of the board with a thin, white cord. Screw two eyelet holes into the back of the board and tie sufficient cord through the eyelets to form a loop for hanging.

Collage pictures The attraction of making collage pictures as a hobby is the flexibility of the materials you can use. You can work with paper or fabric and any other pieces of bric-a-brac you may have to hand, such as braid, lace, sequins, buttons and even tiny shells. A paper collage is probably easier to start with and lends itself well to an abstract design. Choose a piece of firm cardboard as a background and a good clear adhesive. Cut out anything that catches your eye – photographs and advertisements from newspapers and magazines (even a headline or two that amuse you) and you can also use pieces of plain and patterned wrapping papers or tissue or crepe paper. Have a plan of how you are going to arrange the shapes before you start to glue them. Be careful to glue right up to the edges and allow enough time for each piece to dry properly before starting the next. If you want to try a fabric collage choose a firm backing such as canvas or tough cotton or linen, which should be firmly glued to a cardboard base, such as a cake board. Mitre the corners of the canvas or cotton and neatly glue down any excess fabric to the back of the board. If you are going to tackle a realistic subject for your picture you should draw up the shapes carefully then trace them onto tracing paper which then forms the paper pattern from which you cut your fabrics. As with a paper collage use a good, clear adhesive and make sure all

the edges are well glued down. Be as adventurous as you can and let the colours, grains and patterns of fabrics be a feature of your work. Start with simple designs and, as you master the technique, you will be able to tackle more complex subjects. As a rule, try to include areas of plain, bold colour to contrast with the busier designs. Collage is an extremely satisfying hobby in itself and the end results provide you with attractive pictures to hang on your bedroom wall.

Paper flowers It is always nice to have flowers in a room but if you can't treat yourself to a constant supply of the real thing, why not try making paper flowers? They will not provide a permanent display since they fade and get dusty but they do last a lot longer than real flowers. A simple method of making very realistic roses is to use coloured tissues. Fold one tissue in half, with the folded edge at the top. Roll it up and pinch halfway down to form the centre of the rose. Place two more tissues together, fold lengthwise and with the cut edges at the top make two 6 cm cuts down from the top edge. Carefully wind this strip around the rose centre, pinching the bottom together. Now ease out these three petals and with a spoon handle stroke the underside corners of each petal. This will make them curl back realistically. This completes the making of a bud. For a larger bloom add another set of three petals in exactly the same way. Now bind the base of the flower with green wire and cover with green adhesive tape. Make a bowl of roses in varying hues and colour shades and complete by adding sprigs of any suitable natural greenery.

Flower pictures There are two ways of making flower pictures. You can either use a selection of pressed flowers or make a delicate arrangement of dried flowers. The simpler method is to use dried flowers which you can easily purchase from a florist shop or most departmental stores. Use a plain coloured felt as a background and use a tiny dab of rubber solution glue to stick down each of the flowers. Mount in an oval picture or photograph frame for the best effect and hang on a wall in a dry place away from direct sunlight. To make a

pressed flower picture you must first gather and press the flowers you want to use. All you need is a few sheets of white blotting paper and some large books and heavy weights. Try to gather your flowers on a dry day as damp plants go mildewy. Any thick or fleshy plants should not be pressed whole. Gently take them apart and press the petals separately for reassembly when you are making the flower picture. Smooth out the leaves and petals carefully and avoid bruising them. Arrange them between two sheets of blotting paper, allowing plenty of space between each petal and leaf. Place both sheets of blotting paper, with the flowers in between, into your pressing book then keep the book in a dry place heavily weighted down with bricks or other heavy objects. Leave for at least six weeks and DO NOT be tempted to take a peep before they are ready. Choose a piece of thick card on which to mount the flowers and petals and secure each with a tiny smear of rubber solution glue. Do not hang the finished picture in direct sunlight as the colours will fade. If you want to mount your picture behind glass for greater protection, try our extra easy method given below, which saves the need of making or buying a picture frame.

Picture framing A picture frame is not an easy thing to make, and they are usually rather expensive to buy. When a picture is mounted behind glass it always looks better. You can do this quite easily without using a frame. Decide on the overall measurements of your picture after it is mounted on white card, which should allow several inches of white space all around the picture itself. Have a sheet of hardboard and a sheet of glass cut to your chosen dimensions. Place the hardboard, then your mounted picture and finally the glass on top and clip the three together with Swiss clips. Place two clips on each side of the picture near the corners (eight clips altogether). Screw two eyelet holes into the back of the hardboard through which you can thread a length of picture hanging cord. Mirror clips can also be used to secure the glass but the firm backing should be chipboard, which is thick enough for mirror clips to be screwed into – two on each of the edges of the picture.

Indoor Gardening and Flower Arrangements

Care of Indoor Plants

Indoor plants can be an extremely attractive addition to any home and can be just as important to the look of a room as any other accessory. Most plants are very easy to grow as long as you keep to the basic rules. They do not react well to drastic changes in temperature and nothing kills a plant quicker than a draught. Choose a place in the room where the plant can benefit from good indirect light. If they receive direct light, on a windowledge for example, remember to turn the plant regularly, since they will tend to turn their stems and leaves towards the light. If your home is centrally heated you should increase the humidity of the air since hot, dry air can cause discolouration, withering and dropping of the leaves. You can improve the air humidity in close proximity to the plant by occasional misting of the foliage with clean water from a fine-nozzled spray bottle, or stand the pots on a tray of pebbles which is kept damp below the level of the pots. The art of watering is that the soil should never be allowed to dry right out or be so over-watered as to create sodden conditions in which the roots rot. As a rule most plants need watering two to three times a week in summer and in winter only once a week or even fortnightly. If you are not sure of the particular care needed by a specific plant, always refer to one of the many books available on the subject, but most shop-bought plants do give details on how to care for the plant.

If you are interested in plants, flowers and gardening in general looking after indoor plants is a good way to start. You will soon discover if you have 'green fingers' or not, and if everything flourishes well you can gain great enjoyment from growing more spectacular flowers in hanging baskets, garden tubs and window boxes. You may even like to follow our suggestions on how to make a bottle garden or a dish garden.

Families of House Plants

Ivies Exceptionally easy to keep, they provide a wide choice of leaf shapes and sizes, many of which have variegated foliage. Most varieties will either climb or trail.

Ferns Flowerless plants, extremely attractive for the delicacy and beauty of their fronds. They grow well in subdued light.

Cacti and Succulents Slow growing and quite easy to keep providing they are watered too little, rather than too much. Many produce spectacular and colourful flowers.

Coloured Foliage Plants A range of plants whose leaves are of exquisite shapes, colourings and markings. These purely ornamental foliage plants need a lot of light to retain colours which can vary from crimson and maroon to yellow, bronze, brown, green and white.

Figs A rewarding group of plants since they grow quickly. They differ widely in their appearance. Keep away from draughts and be careful not to over-water.

Pepper and Arrowroot Families A small group of plants all originating from the Americas, produce an attractive variety of variegated leaves.

Tradescantias So easy to grow they can survive even if neglected. They grow quickly and are attractive trailing plants bearing small green leaves striped with either silver or pink.

Palms Especially attractive for the overall shape of the plant – need care and benefit from regular sponging of the leaves, or misting with a fine-nozzle spray.

Flowering Shrubs Choose from azalea, poinsettia, passion flower, hydrangea, miniature rose, or even a miniature orange tree (citris mitis). Care according to instructions given when buying plant or look up in a book on the subject.

Spring Bulbs All the spring flowers can be grown successfully as temporary indoor plants. Plant bulbs or corms in flower pots or bowls. While the bulbs are dormant through the winter keep the pots in a dark, cool cupboard. When the flower bud has emerged bring the plant into the light, but keep cool.

Bromeliads All originating from the Americas and the Caribbean islands, they are of exotic and highly decorative appearance. They are hardy plants and survive surprisingly well in low temperatures. The typical form is a rosette of leaves with a cup-like space in the centre which should be kept full of water.

Flowering Annuals Many of the most familiar flowers can be grown indoors, from seed if you wish. They will give colourful displays even though they only flower for a temporary period. Choose from petunias, black-eyed Susan, primulas, nemesia and many others.

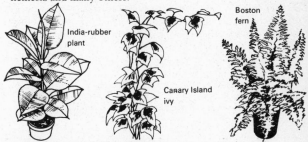

India-rubber plant

Canary Island ivy

Boston fern

Plants Suitable for Window Boxes, Tubs and Hanging Baskets

Ageratum	Lavender	Sweet William
Alyssum	Lobelia	Virginia Stock
Asters	Marguerites	Wallflowers
Aubretia	Marigolds	
Begonias	Mignonette	
Candytuft	Nemesia	*Spring Bulbs*
Cinerarias	Pansies	Crocus
Clarkia	Pelargoniums	Daffodils
Dwarf Dahlias	Petunias	Tulips
Forget-me-nots	Phlox drummondii	Hyacinths
Fuchsias	Snapdragons	Primroses
Geraniums	Stocks	Snowdrops

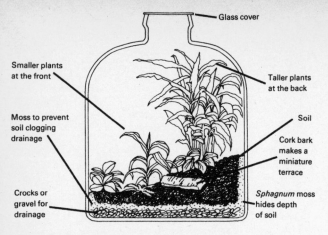

Glass cover

Smaller plants at the front

Taller plants at the back

Moss to prevent soil clogging drainage

Soil

Cork bark makes a miniature terrace

Crocks or gravel for drainage

Sphagnum moss hides depth of soil

Indoor Gardening

If growing flowers and plants appeals to you and you have an artistic flair as well, you may enjoy the challenge of arranging either a dish or bottle garden. Both are extremely attractive and the bottle garden can form the base of a table lamp. First, carefully wash and rinse the bottle and allow to dry thoroughly before planting. You can use any large glass bottle, known as a carboy, or a large cider flagon would do equally well. The soil should consist of two parts loam, one part peat and one part coarse sand with a little charcoal added. It is important to use the correct mixture of soils, all of which can be purchased from any good nursery or gardening shop. Place a layer of crocks or gravel in the bottom to provide drainage, then a layer of moss before pouring the soil into the bottle, using a funnel. You should have the arrangement of the plants already planned before you gently press them through the neck of the bottle. To actually plant them, use two long thin pieces of wood. Give the plants a light watering, using a long-spouted watering can. If the bottle is sealed you need give no further water. The reason watering is not necessary for the survival of plants in a sealed container is that the moisture given off by the leaves, unable to escape into the atmosphere, condenses on the inside of the glass and runs back into the soil to become available for the use of the roots once more. If the bottle is left open give the plants an occasional watering. Our diagram shows a cross-section through a bottle garden. You can see the layers in the soil and a suggested arrangement of plants according to height.

A dish garden can be made in almost any shallow container of approx 10 cm depth. If the container does not have drainage holes you should place a layer of crocks, fine gravel or coarse sand in the bottom of the dish, then a layer of moss, before covering with soil. You can arrange almost any combination of foliage plants and flowering plants and extra accessories can be used in the display, such as pieces of moss-covered bark, interestingly shaped pieces of dead wood or small rocks or pebbles. If the dish garden is going to be placed in a hot, dry room you could try an arrangement of cacti and succulents. Your dish garden will not necessarily be permanent since some of the plants will grow more quickly than others and this could affect the balance and composition of your arrangement.

An attractive
example of a dish garden

Flower Arrangements

Learning how to make beautiful flower arrangements can be the most rewarding of hobbies. Apart from the use of a few basic aids, success lies mainly in the use of imagination and artistic flair. There is scope for the widest variety of end results – arrangements can be simplicity itself or elaborate and formal. This depends on the combination of materials and flowers used, teamed with a container of relevant colour, texture and shape. The height and shape of your arrangement will largely be dictated by the position in the room in which it will be placed. Low and wide for a shelf or windowsill or a full all-round arrangement for a table centre. Colourful accessories can also sometimes be used, for example, pine cones, any attractively shaped twigs and branches, ferns, grasses and even seaweeds.

Stem Holders A pin holder base is most useful – if weighty stems are to be used you should affix the pin holder into the base of the container with blobs of plasticine. Crumpled mesh wire netting will cope with stems of almost any weight and height. As a rule, cut a square twice the diameter of the container, push the sides into the centre and leave the cut ends uppermost so that they can be curled round stems and bent so that the flowers fall in the desired direction. Oasis – a green plastic foam, now much used, makes flower arranging extremely easy. All you do is press in the stems at any angle you want and keep the block of oasis well watered. Plasticine can be used on its own for a dried flower arrangement.

Containers It is possible to use virtually any container that appeals to you, either for its shape, size or texture. You may want a copper container to blend with an autumn arrangement, or a wicker basket to blend with a dried flower arrangement. Consider any of the following – teapots, kettles, cake tins (a loaf tin is particularly good for long, low shapes suitable for window-sills or book shelves). Baskets, jugs, ashtrays, large seashells, soup tureens, gravy boats and any conventional flower containers made either of glass or pottery.

Design and Harmony A simple design is often more effective than a cluttered design. Any combination of flowers and leaves can be tried together. Twigs or branches usually have a pleasing silhouette, so allow space for the outline to be appreciated and balance with a handful of blooms set lower down in the container. Have a shape in mind before you start placing the stems. Always place the centre stem first and work around this focal point. Our diagrams show very simply how this can be done and how to vary the overall shape to balance with the size and shape of the container. Always be prepared to cut stems of flowers. Diagram 2 shows clearly that a short centre stem and longer stems laying horizontally near the container gives a low, wide shape. Diagram 1 shows a conventional half-spherical shape where stems are of a more similar length. Diagram 3 shows a tall, elegant shape by working from the tall centre flower down to the container, using increasingly shorter stems.

Flower arrangements can either be constructed to be viewed from all-round, or just from one side. Diagram 4 shows a side-view arrangement, pretty yet simple, and the dotted line shows the centre, or focal point, of this design.

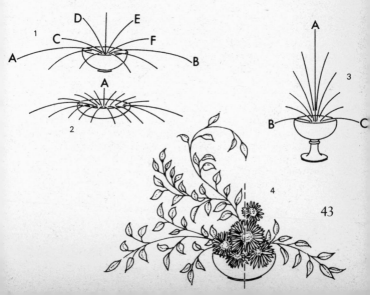

Cookery
Useful Facts and Figures

Basic Methods of Cooking

Baking Cooking in dry heat in the oven.

Boiling Cooking by immersing the food in a pan of liquid, which must be kept boiling gently all the time.

Braising Virtually a combination of stewing and roasting. Meat is placed in a covered container with a little liquid and cooked slowly in the oven.

Casserole Cooking certain cuts of meat that require long, slow cooking in a covered casserole dish with a good quantity of juices or gravy to which vegetables can be added.

Frying Cooking in a little hot fat in an open pan. Deep frying is cooking by immersion in a deep pan of smoking hot fat.

Grilling Cooking quickly under a very hot grill – used for small pieces of tender meat or fish.

Poaching Cooking gently in water which is just below boiling point – generally used for eggs and fish.

Pressure Cooking Cooking at extremely high temperatures under high pressure in a special cooking pot called a pressure cooker. This way food is cooked far more quickly than normal.

Roasting Cooking with a little fat in a hot oven. The meat or poultry is basted from time to time by pouring fat from the baking tray over the meat, using a long handled spoon.

Simmering Cooking food gently just below boiling point, so that the liquid bubbles gently at the side of the pan.

Steaming Cooking either in a steamer over a pan of boiling water, or in a basin standing in (but not covered by) boiling water.

Stewing Cooking slowly until the food is tender, with just enough liquid to cover the food. A stew can be cooked on a burner or in the oven, but always at a low temperature.

44

Oven Temperatures

The following chart gives conversions from degrees Fahrenheit to degrees Celsius (formerly known as Centigrade).

Description	Electric Setting	Gas Mark
Very cool	225°F–110°C	$\frac{1}{4}$
	250°F–130°C	$\frac{1}{2}$
Cool	275°F–140°C	1
	300°F–150°C	2
Moderate	325°F–170°C	3
	350°F–180°C	4
Moderately hot	375°F–190°C	5
	400°F–200°C	6
Hot	425°F–220°C	7
	450°F–230°C	8
Very hot	475°F–240°C	9

This table is an approximate guide only. Different makes of cooker vary. If in doubt about the setting refer to manufacturer's temperature chart.

Useful Tips on Metrication For quick and easy reference when buying food, remember that 1 kilogramme (1,000 grammes) equals 2.2 pounds (35¾ ounces) i.e. as a rough guide, ½ kilogramme (500 grammes) is about 1 pound. In liquid measurements 1 litre (10 decilitres or 1,000 millilitres) equals almost exactly 1¾ pints, so ½ litre is ⅞ pint. As a rough guide therefore, assume that the equivalent of 1 pint is a generous ½ litre. A simple method of converting recipe quantities, and one which is used in many cookery books, is to use round figures instead of an exact conversion, working to an equivalent of 25 grammes to 1 ounce and a generous ½ litre to 1 pint.

Metrication Conversion Charts
Dry Ingredients

Imperial **Ounces**	(Exact conversion to nearest whole number) **Grammes**	(Recommended equivalent) **Grammes**
1	28	25
2	57	50
3	85	75
4	113	100
5	142	125
6	170	150
7	198	175
8	226	200

Liquids

Imperial **Pints**	(Exact conversion to nearest dl = decilitre) **Millilitres**	(Recommended equivalent) **Litres**
1 pint (20 fl oz)	568 (6 dl)	½ litre (generous)
¾ pint	426 (4½ dl)	⅜ litre (generous)
½ pint	284 (3 dl)	¼ litre (generous)
¼ pint	142 (1½ dl)	⅛ litre (generous)
1 fl oz	28	25 ml

HANDICRAFTS

Embroidery

Running stitch An easy stitch depending for effect on its regularity. Pass the needle over and under the fabric making both the upper and lower stitches of equal length. The upper stitches should be twice the length of the under stitches (1).

Back stitch This stitch gives an unbroken outline. Work from right to left. Bring the thread through on the stitch line then take a small backward stitch through the fabric. Bring the needle through again a little in front of the first stitch, take another stitch, inserting the needle at the point where it first came through (2).

Stem stitch A stitch widely used for embroidering flower stems and outlines since it goes round curves very well, especially if the stitches are small. Work from left to right. Regular, slightly slanting stitches are made along the line of the design, with the thread always emerging on the left side of the previous stitch (3).

Straight stitch Simple and useful in many designs, it consists of single spaced stitches which can be worked in either a regular or irregular manner. Take care not to make the stitches too long or loose (4).

Satin stitch Excellent for filling in small shapes. Bring the needle up at one edge of the design. Insert at opposite edge and return to starting edge by carrying the thread underneath the fabric. Stitches should be parallel and close together (5).

Long and short stitch A form of satin stitch, working both long and short stitches. Useful for filling in larger areas and good for shading when two colours are used (6).

Herringbone stitch Work from left to right, but insert needle from right. Make a diagonal stitch then take a very short stitch next to it. Bring needle down to form another diagonal stitch crossing over the first one. Alternate up and down stitches (7).

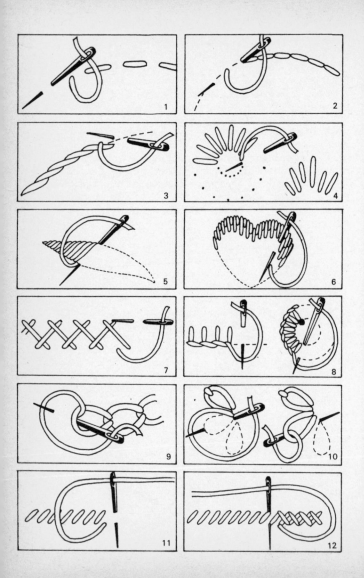

Blanket and buttonhole stitch Both stitches are worked in the same way, except to make a buttonhole the stitches are worked close together. Work from left to right. Bring needle up on lower line. Hold thread down with left thumb. Insert needle a little to the right of the starting point but on the upper line. Bring out directly below on the lower line. Draw needle through and over the loop of thread (8).

Chain stitch Bring needle to right side of fabric. Hold thread down with left thumb. Insert needle back where thread emerged and bring out a short distance away. Draw needle over loop (9).

Lazy Daisy stitch A quick way of working flowers and leaves. Bring thread up in the centre of the flower. Hold thread down with left thumb, insert needle where thread emerged and bring out at the desired distance (length of petal or leaf). Draw needle over thread and secure with a tiny stitch made over the loop (10).

Cross stitch Work in rows across the design from left to right, keeping needle straight between the two lines of the cross. To make half the cross, make diagonal stitches to upper right corner. To make second half, work from right to left (11/12).

Feather stitch This gives a pretty, lacy effect. Bring the needle out at the centre top, hold the thread down with left thumb, insert the needle a little to the right on the same level and take a small stitch down to the centre, keeping the thread under the needle point. Next, insert the needle a little to the left on the same level and take a stitch to the centre, keeping the thread under the needle point. Work two stages alternately (13).

French knots A good way of making small dots for flower stamens. Bring thread out at required position, hold thread down with left thumb and encircle the thread twice round the needle. Hold thread firmly, twist needle back to the starting point and insert it close to where the thread first emerged. Pass thread through to back and secure (14).

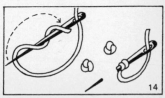

Knitting

It is important to remember, whatever stitch you are knitting, always to hold the needles correctly. Hold the needle in your left hand between your fingers and thumb, resting it against your palm. On the right, rest the needle on top of your hand between your thumb and first finger. When working stitches the wool lays across the top of the first finger of the right hand and is held firmly by looping it under the second finger. In this way the wool is conveniently secured for passing the wool around the right hand needle when creating new stitches.

Casting on Take a ball of wool and make a loop 10 cm (4 inches) from end. Push right-hand needle into stitch (1). Loop wool around point of right-hand needle and draw between the two needles (2). With point of right-hand needle draw wool through the stitch on the left-hand needle. You have now created a new stitch on the right-hand needle (3). Transfer new stitch from right-hand to left-hand needle (4). Continue to make more stitches in this way until you have the correct number. These four diagrams also clearly show how the needles and wool should be held, as described in the first paragraph.

Plain stitch Push the point of the right-hand needle through the first stitch on the left-hand needle from left to right. Wind

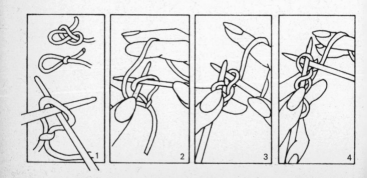

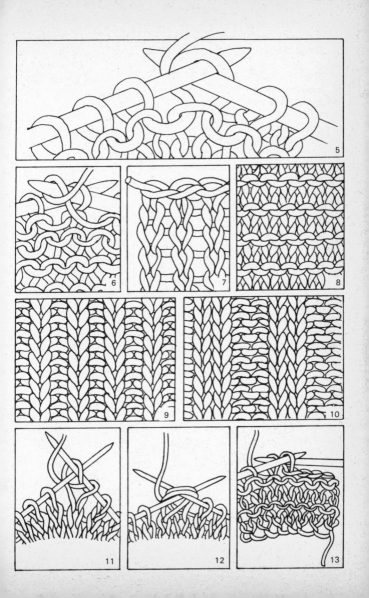

wool once around the right-hand needle. Draw loop through stitch on left-hand needle and slip new stitch onto the right-hand needle. Continue to end of row. Turn round needle holding stitches and knit the next row (5).

Purl stitch Keep wool and right-hand needle to front of work. Push point of right-hand needle through front of first stitch on the left-hand needle from right to left. Wrap wool once round right-hand needle taking it over the top of the needle first. Keeping loop in place, draw right-hand needle through stitch on left-hand needle and slip new stitch onto the right-hand needle. Continue to end of row (6).

Stocking stitch The most commonly used stitch in knitting, this consists, very simply, of alternating one row of purl and one row of plain knitting (7).

Garter stitch Plain stitch every row. This gives a heavier appearance, in contrast to the flat finish on the right side of stocking stitch (8).

Ribbing This consists of alternating plain and purl stitches on the same row. It makes a good, firm border around the bottom of jumpers and for cuffs and polo necks. Always work with an even number of stitches in the row. You can choose between single rib (one knit, one purl) or double rib (two knit, two purl) (9 and 10).

To shape garments it is always necessary to increase (11) and decrease (12) the number of stitches on the needles and finally it is necessary to cast off (13).

Increasing Knit the stitch in the normal way, but before slipping it off the left-hand needle push the point of the right-hand needle through the back of the same stitch and knit it again. Now slip the extra stitch onto the right-hand needle.

Decreasing Knit two stitches together.

Casting-off Knit two stitches. Using the point of the left-hand needle lift the first stitch knitted over the second stitch and slip off needle. Knit next stitch on left-hand needle and repeat the process. Continue until you have one stitch remaining. Break wool, draw through final stitch and pull firmly.

52

Crochet

The first loop To start crocheting, hold hook in one hand and loop yarn over hook in open knot with other hand. With thumb and forefinger pull yarn gently to tighten (1).

How to hold work Hold the hook as you would a pencil, but do not hold too tightly. Keep yarn away from work while crocheting by looping the long thread round the little finger of your left hand, then across the palm and behind the forefinger (2) and (3).

Chain stitch The foundation of all crochet work. With yarn in position and first loop on hook, pass hook under the yarn (held between the forefinger of the left hand and hook), catch yarn with hook (4) and draw through to make a loop (5). Repeat until you have as many chain stitches as you need.

Slip stitch or single crochet Used to give a firm edge or for joining, fastening or re-positioning yarn without adding to the dimensions of the work. Insert the hook into the stitch below to the left of the hook, catch the long thread and draw it through the stitch and the loop already on the hook. This forms a flat chain (6).

Double crochet Insert the hook into the stitch to the left of the hook (under both top loops of the stitch) and catch yarn with hook (7). Draw yarn through stitch. There are now two loops on the hook (8). Put the yarn over the hook and draw it through the two loops, leaving one loop on the hook (9).

Half treble Pass the hook under the yarn held in the left hand, insert the hook into the stitch to the left of the hook. Catch the yarn and draw it through the stitch. This makes three loops on the hook. Put yarn over hook (10) and draw it through all loops on hook, leaving one loop on hook (11).

Treble crochet Pass the hook under yarn held in left hand, insert the hook into the stitch to the left of the hook and draw yarn through, making three loops on the hook. Put the yarn over the hook again (12) and pull it through the first two loops on the hook, leaving two loops on the hook. Put the yarn over

53

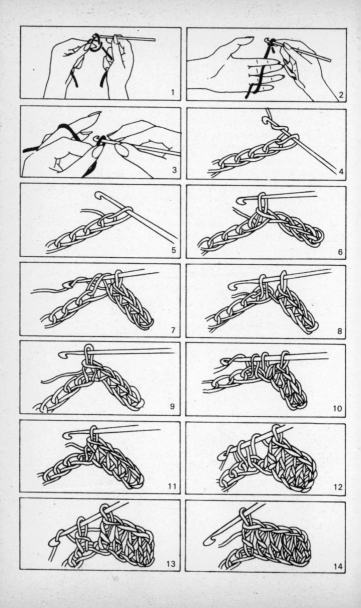

the hook once more (13) and draw through the last two loops, leaving one loop on hook (14).

Double treble Pass the hook under the yarn twice, put the hook into the next stitch, put yarn over the hook and pull it through the stitch, to give four loops on the hook (15). Put the yarn over the hook and pull it through two loops, leaving three loops, then put yarn over hook again and pull through the next two loops. Finally put yarn over the hook again and pull through the last two loops.

Picot Work a chain of three, four or five stitches, depending on the size of picot required. Form into a loop by working one double crochet into foundation of first chain (16).

To complete crochet Cut off thread, leaving approximately 15 cm (6 inches). Insert hook into final loop and pull through last loop. Pull yarn end to tighten. Thread excess yarn into a bodkin needle, work it back into the piece of crochet down the edge and cut off close to work.

To join two edges Place edges side by side, matching stitches perfectly. Insert hook under two yarns of first stitch of both edges (under four yarns). Put yarn over hook, draw yarn through these stitches and the loop on the hook. Repeat movement through next pair of stitches.

If you are left handed Simply follow all the instructions reading right for left and left for right. You can look at the diagrams reflected in a mirror to see them in reverse.

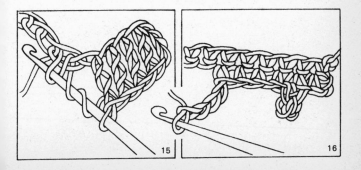

Dressmaking

Dressmaking is something most girls want to try their hand at. The whole aim, of course, is to produce a garment you will enjoy wearing. To start with, make life easy for yourself – choose a simple pattern such as an A-line skirt or pinafore dress and use an easy-to-work-with fabric. If you do this there will be a far greater chance of achieving a good result that you will be pleased with. Gradually, with confidence and success you will be able to advance to greater things. Having chosen the pattern and fabric you must then be prepared to be careful and organised in your approach to making up the garment. Do not hurry and rush at it because haste leads to mistakes and inevitable frustration at having to unpick seams and start again – and there's no satisfaction in that! So, take your time and carry out each stage carefully according to the instructions given on the pattern.

Pattern Fitting The first step is choosing your pattern according to figure type. It is useful to make out a chart, such as the one shown here, which specifies all the measuring points on your body. Having bought your pattern you can enter in the pattern measurements and you will know the areas where any adjustments will be necessary. If you can learn at the beginning the art of adjusting patterns to fit, you will be well on the way to being a good dressmaker. A garment will never look good if there are pulls and wrinkles or it is obviously too tight or loose. If you have a deviation from the normal figure measurements this will usually occur in one area only. Certain adjustments, such as extra length and width, should obviously be made at the pattern stage before cutting out. Other things, such as adjusting to sloping shoulders or a small bust can be made at the first fitting stage when you are free to adjust seams and darts.

When comparing pattern measurements to your own it is important to bear in mind that all patterns are designed to fit with ease – they should neither fit so loosely they hide the natural line of the figure, or so tightly they pull or cause rucks on any of the

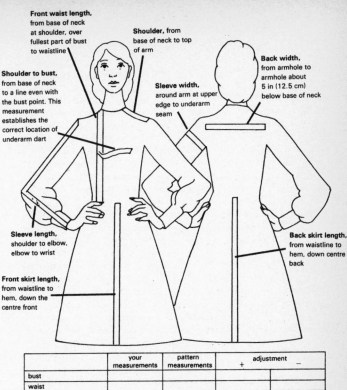

Front waist length, from base of neck at shoulder, over fullest part of bust to waistline

Shoulder, from base of neck to top of arm

Shoulder to bust, from base of neck to a line even with the bust point. This measurement establishes the correct location of underarm dart

Sleeve width, around arm at upper edge to underarm seam

Back width, from armhole to armhole about 5 in (12.5 cm) below base of neck

Sleeve length, shoulder to elbow, elbow to wrist

Back skirt length, from waistline to hem, down centre back

Front skirt length, from waistline to hem, down the centre front

	your measurements	pattern measurements	adjustment +	adjustment −
bust				
waist				
hips				
back waist length				
back bodice width				
shoulder				
front waist length				
shoulder to bust				
sleeve width				
front skirt length				
back skirt length				
sleeve, shoulder to elbow				
sleeve, elbow to wrist				

fitting points. Once you have analysed your figure problems and have learnt to make the correct adjustments at the right stage you will have the guidelines, not only for your first, but all future dressmaking projects and it will be quite a simple matter for you to produce clothes that fit perfectly first time. A good tip, if you have to make adjustments at the fitting stage is to put the garment on inside out so that the seams and darts can easily be worked on.

Cutting Out Cutting out a pattern needs to be done carefully. First of all, remove all the pattern pieces from the envelope and select the pieces you will require, depending on which view of the garment you have decided to make. You will then follow the laying out diagram for that view given on the instruction sheet. All pattern pieces allow a tissue margin which you should not cut off unless you are working with a very heavy or slippery fabric. Now press the wrinkles out of the paper pattern with a warm, dry iron. Do not steam iron a pattern as this could make the paper tissue shrink. You should also press the fabric if it has noticeable folds and creases from being stored. With all lengths of fabric test to see that the centre fold will iron out by using a steam iron and pressing on the crosswise grain.

When you buy fabric it is usually folded in half on the lengthwise grain with the right sides together (on the inside of the fold) and the selvage edges meeting. Follow the laying out diagram exactly and place all pattern pieces down before cutting, starting by pinning pieces that are placed on the fold. Pay special attention to arrows on pattern pieces which indicate the direction in which a piece should be placed, according to the grain. A pattern can require a combination of crosswise, lengthwise and bias grains. Now pin the pieces to the fabric. Pin at right angles to the cutting edge and do not allow the pinpoints to extend beyond the cutting edge. Place them 6–8 inches (15 cm–20 cm) apart and pin diagonally into corners. Smooth out the pattern pieces as you go to eliminate pulls and wrinkles and only pick up a few threads with each pin so that the pattern and fabric lie flat. Cut out pattern pieces with long, firm strokes of the scissors (preferably bent-handled shears, as described in 'Sewing Equipment'). Use shorter strokes for cutting around curves. Hold the fabric flat on the table by placing your left hand on the fabric near to the edge of the pattern. Cut notches outward and if a pattern piece has been pinned on a fold make a tiny snip at either end to mark the centre. You can use the selvage for the straight edge of a pattern piece but if, after washing, it becomes tight or pulled, snip the selvage at intervals to release the tension.

Leave all pattern pieces attached to fabric ready for you to transfer all the markings.

Transferring Markings It is important to transfer the markings or construction symbols from the pattern to the wrong side of the garment pieces. These markings are your guide for sewing the garment shaping and details, and must be done both neatly and accurately. It is not necessary to mark the lines indicating the normal seam allowance.

When marking darts you must mark both the stitching lines and the line through the centre, known as the fold line. As an additional help, make a line at right angles to the point of the dart. This gives a clear visible guide for the end of the dart when the fabric is folded prior to stitching.

Other markings should also be transferred, such as position lines for buttonholes, pocket locations and so on. These should be transferred to the wrong side of the fabric, then clearly shown on the front of the fabric by basting along the lines either by hand or machine. If you are making a pleated skirt the line of the pleats should be marked down the whole length of the skirt. You should also make a clear mark at the point where the stitching ends and the pleat opening begins.

One method for transferring markings is to use a dressmakers' tracing wheel and tracing paper (see section on sewing equipment). Insert small piece of tracing paper, coated side down, between the pattern and fabric, removing pins where necessary.

To mark two thicknesses of fabric, with right sides together, use a strip of tracing paper folded with the coated sides together. Insert one end under bottom layer of fabric, the other end between the pattern and top layer of fabric. Using a clear ruler as a guide, mark the straight centre line of a dart first to prevent the pattern from sliding as you work. Now mark the two outside lines in the same manner, always pushing the tracing wheel away from you.

Chalk and pins is another method. Push small-headed pins straight through the tissue and both layers of fabric. When all the points are marked, turn the fabric over so that the points of the pins face upwards. Now, using a transparent ruler and a fine-pointed chalk pencil, draw straight lines connecting all the points. Turn the fabric over again, so that the pattern is once again uppermost. Carefully remove the pattern over the pin

A dart marked by using a dressmaker's tracing wheel and tracing paper

Position lines for button-holes and pockets should be basted onto front of fabric

Chalk and pin method, using a transparent ruler and a fine-pointed chalk pencil

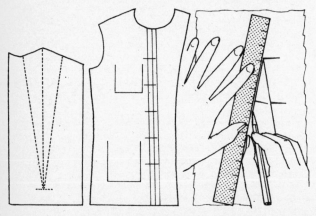

heads and, with ruler and chalk pencil, draw a line connecting the pin heads. Now the pins can be removed.

Tailor's tacks are a particularly good method if you are using heavyweight, bulky or lacy fabrics. Use a long, double unknotted thread. Work tacks at each of the dots along a marking line. Take a small stitch through the pattern and both fabric layers. The stitch should not be pulled tight, but done loosely enough to form a loop. Cut thread leaving approximately 2–3 cm (1 inch) either side of the loop. Cut through top of loops and then remove pattern so as not to pull out the threads. Separate the two layers of fabric, cutting the threads between. You will now have tufts of cotton marking both pattern pieces.

Sewing Before starting the stitching of a garment it is always sensible to test stitch length, pressure and tension on a scrap of the same material. These factors are dictated by the weight and texture of the fabric. Having established the correct settings on your sewing machine you are ready to start sewing.

Pressing Pressing is a very important factor in giving a garment a well-made look and professional finish. This doesn't mean just giving it a final press. You should be prepared to press as you work. If seams and darts of one section are pressed smooth before sewing it to another garment section, the following sewing stage is made a lot easier. This method is called 'construction pressing' and is well worth the little extra time it takes.

Again, it is wise to do a test with the iron on a scrap of fabric to see how much heat, pressure and moisture will be required. As a rule most pressing will be done on the wrong side of the garment and extra care is needed when pressing on the right side to avoid iron shine. Use a steam iron cloth to avoid this. Pressing hems always need especial care. To avoid pressing the hem line through to the front of the fabric, place a piece of the same material right up to the hemline. Do not push the iron over the hem, but lift and press from section to section. Always work from hem edge to folded edge.

Equipment

The Sewing machine Assuming you have the use of a sewing machine, an ordinary straight stitch machine is quite adequate for straightforward work. Most will have a zipper foot attachment. The type of refinements you will find on a modern swing-needle (zig-zag) machine will enable you to do certain jobs more easily and swiftly. The zig-zag will oversew and finish seam edges so that awkward fabrics cannot fray. Usually stretch stitches are included, which means all the modern stretch fabrics can be sewn successfully. A sophisticated machine can usually do a range of more intricate jobs such as smocking, quilting and so on, but lack of these refinements need not put you off, especially if you are a beginner tackling relatively simple designs. If you are lucky enough to have an elaborate zig-zag machine to use, do not let it give you grand ideas. A complicated machine takes time to know before you can make full use of its attributes! So, keep things simple, and make use of the zig-zag for finishing seams and learn how to use the zipper and buttonhole attachments properly.

Cutting equipment Try to use a really good pair of bent-handled shears – 7–8 inches (18–20 cm) in length being the most popular size. 'Bent-handled' are best because the blade rests flat on the cutting surface and you do not have to lift the fabric to cut around the pattern. A pair of sewing and embroidery scissors – 4–5 inches (10–12 cm) in length have thin, pointed blades and are good for detail jobs such as cutting odd threads and cutting buttonhole slits. A seam ripper is a particularly useful small tool which makes unpicking seams a far quicker job. Use with care as it is easy to catch or cut the fabric.

Measuring equipment Use a good tape measure made of a fabric that will not stretch or tear. Choose one that is marked on both sides, is a full 60 inches long (1.5 metres) and has a metal tip at each end. Various other measuring devices such as skirt markers and hem gauges exist but only bother to get these if you are going in for dressmaking in a big way. A mother or friend will always be able to help you when a garment reaches the final hemming stage.

Marking aids Dressmaker's tracing or carbon paper is used to transfer markings from pattern to fabric or linings. Choose a colour either lighter or darker than that of the fabric you are using. A pack of assorted colours is useful to have. A transparent ruler is essential to use with a tracing wheel or chalk pencil for marking lines of pattern alterations, darts, pleats or any straight line markings. Tailors' chalk and chalk pencils are used when tracing paper cannot be used. The pencils are the easiest to use since they can be sharpened to a fine point and give a thin, accurate line. A tracing wheel with teeth or dull points should be used with carbon paper. Place a piece of cardboard underneath your fabric before you start. This will protect your working surface and give you a better impression off the carbon paper.

Other equipment Use fine, non-rusting dressmaking pins, a pin cushion with an elastic holder so that it will stay conveniently on your wrist and have a thimble handy if you are pinning or sewing through very thick or several thicknesses of fabric.

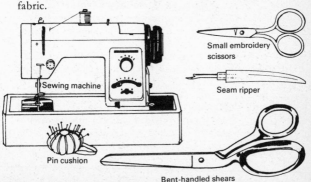

Sewing machine

Small embroidery scissors

Seam ripper

Pin cushion

Bent-handled shears

Applique

You can applique a motif onto almost anything you feel needs a facelift, and the technique is extremely simple. In recent years it has been a point of fashion to have bright, bold motifs on clothes and accessories of all sorts. Although it is mainly used as a decorative addition to clothes it can be fun to set a motif on a patch to hide worn areas, such as the knees or seat of a favourite old pair of jeans. Once you start you will find you will have plenty of ideas. A motif can be one single shape, such as a sun, star, flower or fruit or you can create a simple picture such as a house with tree, sun or rainbow arranged around it.

Have a good look through your wardrobe – if there's anything you have tired of or feel needs brightening up you can well give it a new lease of life. Or if you feel doubtful until you have tried the technique once or twice, you could make a start by doing an applique design on a plain cushion cover.

There are two methods – either stitching the motif on by hand or by using the zig-zag stitch on a swing needle sewing machine.

Method and materials Have plenty of odd scraps of material to hand. As a rule it is best to match the weight of the materials – that is the motif should be the same weight as fabric onto which it will be stitched. Avoid slippery fabrics or ones that will fray, ladder or stretch. You will also need a needle and embroidery silks if you intend to attach the motif with a fancy embroidery stitch, or you may want to embroider a few details on the motif – such as pips on a strawberry or scales on a fish. Small, sharp scissors are essential for cutting round the shapes. You will also need pins and pencil, rubber and tracing paper for working out your designs.

Having drawn your design carefully onto the tracing paper, use this as a pattern, pin to fabric and cut out the motif. If any embroidery detail is needed, do it at this stage. If you are using a swing needle sewing machine, baste the motif in place and stitch with closely spaced zig-zag stitch (so close it looks like satin stitch) around the outline, but approximately ½ inch (1.3 cm) in from the outer edge. Remove basting stitches, press and trim off the excess border of fabric outside the zig-zag stitching, as close to stitching as possible.

If you are going to stitch the motif on by hand, when you cut out the design, leave a ¼ inch (6 mm) allowance for turning. Outline the shape with normal machine straight stitching then clip notches on all outside curved edges, using the ¼ inch allowance. Now turn under this allowance to include the outline of machine stitching. Baste the motif in place and you can either use an invisible slip-stitch or a decorative embroidery stitch to attach the design permanently in position. If you want to give depth to your applique you can gently press a piece of terylene wadding under the applique before finishing the edge stitching.

It is also possible to buy ready-made iron-on applique shapes, but these can work out to be rather expensive. It is more fun to be adventurous and imaginative and make your own motifs. If you want a really personal touch you could settle on one design for everything you want to brighten up – to show that it is yours.

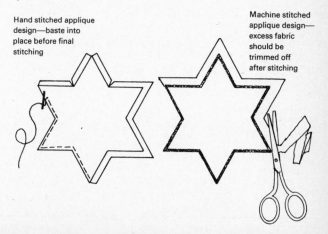

Hand stitched applique design—baste into place before final stitching

Machine stitched applique design—excess fabric should be trimmed off after stitching

Patchwork

Patchwork is a delightful craft which has been popular for generations. It is possible to create totally individual results according to the shapes and variety of colours and designs of fabrics used. Generally used to produce home furnishing items such as cushion covers and bedspreads, although the patchwork look has become popular in the world of fashion and can be used in dressmaking – to create a colourful bodice or pockets or as a border let into a skirt or dress.

Fabrics Although you can use most fabrics it is certainly best to keep to crisp cottons, especially if you are a beginner. Cotton is easy to handle, the turnings press down well and, of course, is trouble free to wash and iron. Never use a different mixture of textures and thicknesses in one piece of work since the work will pucker and not lie flat. Avoid fabrics that fray or ones that are slippery as they are difficult to handle.

Templates You can make your own or buy ready-made templates from craft shops. Two sets of templates are required of the same shape – the stiff card template which you use as a pattern for cutting out the fabric pieces and paper lining templates onto which you tack each of the fabric shapes. The paper template determines the finished size of the shapes and should be at least $\frac{1}{4}$ inch (6 mm) smaller all round than the cutting template. Templates can be square, diamond shaped, triangular or hexagonal. The hexagonal shape is the best for a beginner to use since the corners are not as sharp as on diamonds and squares, and are a lot easier to handle.

Mark and cut out very accurately as many paper lining templates as required – that is, one for each of patches you will be using. Use firm, crisp paper such as scraps of wallpaper or brown parcel paper. Avoid glossy paper that will slip around.

Having cut out as many fabric shapes as required the next stage is to place a paper lining centrally on the wrong side of each fabric patch and pin. Make a small tuck at each corner, fold over edge of fabric onto paper and tack all round fabric shape as accurately as possible. Now you can start to join the patches together, working to your plan (from the centre out). With right sides together, hold two patches together and oversew the edges using neat, tiny stitches. Try not to sew through the paper linings. Ensure that all corners join exactly so that the finished work will lie flat. Continue until your design is completed then carefully remove all the tacking threads and take out the paper linings (which can be re-used). Press the completed work on the wrong side so that all turnings lie flat and smooth, each pointing towards the centre of the patch. Finally, back your work with a suitable, washable fabric which should always be pre-shrunk to avoid puckering. Choose from sheeting, curtain-lining or any medium weight plain fabric.

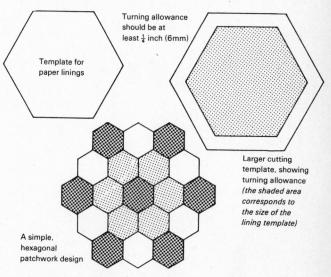

Template for paper linings

Turning allowance should be at least $\frac{1}{4}$ inch (6mm)

Larger cutting template, showing turning allowance *(the shaded area corresponds to the size of the lining template)*

A simple, hexagonal patchwork design

Cushion covers The diagrams show two plans for making cushion covers – one using strips of fabric and the other using diamond shapes. The hexagonal shapes, shown on the previous page, give a hexagonal shape to the finished cushion itself, whereas the diamond shapes provide a circular cushion – with the final round of shapes being triangular (use half the diamond shape for these). When working with diamond templates a second fold is required at each of the four sharp corners when tacking the fabric over the paper lining template. Always make a cushion cover the exact size of the cushion itself to ensure a full, plump cushion. For the back of the cushion use a fabric that will tone with the general colour scheme of the patchwork front. Stitch back and front of cushion together with wrong sides facing and with neat hand stitching oversew the edges together leaving a gap for the cushion pad to be placed inside. Finally, oversew this gap and finish the edges with a plain piping.

Strips of fabric can be used to make a cushion cover which is, of course, a very quick and simple method compared to working with more complex shapes. However, if you enjoy the craft, you may well want to attempt a bedcover. With a project of such large dimensions it is possible to have a much more complex design using a combination of shapes, sizes of shapes and work varying panels and borders to achieve an attractive and individual overall design.

Two cushion cover designs. Diamond shapes used for making a circular cushion. Strips of fabric, the quickest method for making a square cushion.

HOBBIES

Signs of the Zodiac

ARIES March 21–April 20. *Personality:* Lively and extrovert. You need to get out and about and meet people, know what is going on and join in. You also have a tendency to be impulsive and quick tempered, so be careful not to hurt people. *Careers:* Since you have a lot of drive and enthusiasm, the sort of qualities people need to get to the top, choose a job that gives scope for progress and where you can use your

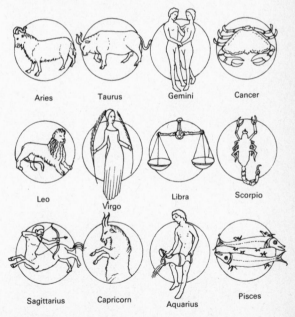

Aries

Taurus

Gemini

Cancer

Leo

Virgo

Libra

Scorpio

Sagittarius

Capricorn

Aquarius

Pisces

initiative. *Compatible signs:* Leo and Sagittarius are other fire signs that you should get along well with, also the intellectual signs of Gemini, Libra and Aquarius. *Luck:* You have true beginner's luck and do well out of new ideas. *Ruling planet:* The fiery planet Mars gives you energy and drive. *Lucky number:* 9; *Day* – Tuesday; *Colours* – Red and White; *Metals* – Iron and Steel; *Gems* – Diamond, Crystal and Bloodstone.

TAURUS April 21–May 20.
Personality: Placid, sociable and affectionate by nature, you are also artistic and enjoy being in nice surroundings. *Careers:* You have a special magnetism which seems to give strength to others so choose some form of healing work such as nursing or physiotherapy. *Compatible signs:* The signs of Cancer, Virgo, Scorpio and Capricorn are the best for you since they have similar intentions to your own. *Luck:* You seem to draw the good things in life to you. You enjoy material comfort and attain and enjoy the luxuries in life easily. *Ruling planet:* Venus, the planet that makes life easy for you. *Lucky number:* 6; *Day* – Friday; *Colours* – Pastel Blues, Pinks, Green and Beige; *Metal* – Copper; *Gems* – Ruby, Diamond and Sapphire.

GEMINI May 21–June 20.
Personality: Inquisitive, friendly and talkative by nature, you love to know what's going on. Since you learn quickly, you easily get bored. Movement and changes are essential to you. *Careers:* Travel, communications, teaching, writing and broadcasting are all good possibilities for you. *Compatible signs:* Other people of your own sign, plus Libra and Aquarius. *Luck:* You are lucky in Mercurial things such as publications and transport. Butterflies are also lucky for Gemini people, so wear a butterfly brooch or pendant. *Ruling planet:* Mercury, the planet of articulation and communication. *Lucky number:* 5; *Day* – Wednesday; *Colours* – Yellow and pale Grey; *Metal* – Quicksilver; *Gems* – Emerald, Agate and Sapphire.

CANCER June 21–July 20.
Personality: Sensitive and Romantic. You are intuitive and instinctively know what is needed in a given situation. Although you are homely and protective you can be shrewd in politics and money matters.

70

Careers: Your emotional drive should help you in such jobs as nursing, public welfare and running a home and family. Cancer is also a strong sign for acting and writing. *Compatible signs:* Pisces, Taurus, Scorpio, Capricorn and other Cancerians. *Luck:* You are tenacious and can succeed in spite of fluctuating conditions. Your natural love of history and all things old can make you lucky in antiques. *Ruling planet:* The Moon which will bring you many changes in life. *Lucky number:* 2; *Day* – Monday; *Colours* – Violet, Mauve, Silver and Grey; *Metal* – Silver; *Gems* – Moonstone, Agate, Emerald and Pearls.

LEO July 21–August 21.

Personality: You have a warm, friendly personality. You get on well with people influential and enjoy holding authority. You are a good organiser and a born leader, although inclined to be a bit of a show-off on occasions. *Careers:* Choose jobs where your personality will come to the fore, such as show business, public relations, the hotel and travel trades. *Compatible signs:* Aries, Libra, Sagittarius, Aquarius and other Leos. *Luck:* Your luck lies in your social life and knowing the right person at the right time. *Ruling planet:* The Sun, giver of all life. *Lucky number:* 1; *Day* – Sunday; *Colours* – Yellow, Green and Orange; *Metal* – Gold; *Gems* – Ruby, Onyx, Agate and Topaz.

VIRGO August 22–September 22.

Personality: You are observant and a perfectionist and very conscious of detail. You are always ready to analyse, compare and criticise, so you must make an effort to be constructive in your comments, rather than negative. *Careers:* You are a natural as a teacher or secretary. Your ability to impart information in a clear and concise fashion is your strongest point. You could do well in research. *Compatible signs:* Capricorn, Libra, Cancer, Pisces, Scorpio and Taurus. *Luck:* Your luck lies in your passion for detail, which is said to be nine-tenths of genius' make-up. *Ruling planet:* Mercury, planet of communication, quick-thinking and articulation. *Lucky number:* 5; *Day* – Wednesday; *Colours* – Orange, Brown and Greens; *Metal* – Mercury, also Silver and Platinum; *Gems* – Jade, Cornelian, Sardonyx.

LIBRA September 23–October 22. *Personality:* You have great natural charm and are happy and at ease with others. You are extremely likeable but inclined to be lazy. *Careers:* You enjoy a sociable job in pleasing surroundings, so choose to work with beautiful people and beautiful things. Modelling, art, music, public relations and reception work could all suit you. *Compatible signs:* Gemini, Sagittarius, Leo, Aquarius and other Librans. *Luck:* You frequently have the gift of good looks and your luck lies in your personal charm. *Ruling planet:* Venus, giver of luck, love and money. *Lucky number:* 6; *Day –* Friday; *Colours –* Soft Blue, Grey and Pink; *Metal –* Copper; *Gems –* Turquoise and Sapphire.

SCORPIO October 23–November 22. *Personality:* You are intense, strong-minded and determined to live life on your own terms. You are inclined to be possessive and jealous and you should curb your instincts to dominate others. *Careers:* You have a good mind for such jobs as research, medicine, the sciences in general. You could also be good in police, nursing and welfare jobs. *Compatible signs:* Pisces, Cancer, Scorpio and Taurus, also Virgo and Capricorn. *Luck:* You have a magnetic personality and often have luck in money matters. *Ruling planet:* Mars, which gives you energy and drive. *Lucky number:* 9; *Day –* Tuesday; *Colours –* Red; *Metals –* Iron and Steel; *Gems –* Opal, Bloodstone, Topaz and Beryl.

SAGITTARIUS November 23–December 20. *Personality:* You are gay and active, an extrovert who makes friends easily and loves to live a restless life. You are honest and straightforward. *Careers:* Journalism, market research, travel and outdoor jobs in general. Higher education can also have a strong appeal for you. *Compatible signs:* Aries, Leo, Sagittarius, Gemini, Libra or Aquarius. *Luck:* You are lucky with your friends since your generous and open nature attracts other similar people. *Ruling planet:* Jupiter, giver of good fortune. *Lucky number:* 3; *Day –* Thursday; *Colours –* Royal Blue, Purple, Mauve, Turquoise, Emerald Green; *Metal –* Tin; *Gems –* Amethyst, Garnet, Ruby, Topaz.

CAPRICORN December 21—January 19. *Personality:* Serious, studious and essentially ambitious, you expect to work hard, but hope to get to the top. You are not openly gregarious, preferring to have just one or two special friends to whom you are loyal and helpful. *Careers:* Avoid high-powered jobs, instead go for a job where your reliability and conscientious work will be valued highly. Choose employment in government and old-established firms. *Compatible signs:* Virgo, Taurus, Cancer, Pisces and Scorpio. *Luck:* You have a long life expectancy. *Ruling planet:* Saturn, which brings you security. *Lucky number:* 8; *Day* – Saturday; *Colours* – Grey, Brown, Black and Dark Green and Blue; *Metal* – Lead and Pewter; *Gems* – Garnet, Sapphire, Turquoise, Ruby and Jet.

AQUARIUS January 20—February 18. *Personality:* You are friendly in a detached way, preferring to mix with a group of acquaintances rather than sticking to one close friend. *Careers:* You need interesting and progressive work. Advertising, script-writing, acting, travel and socially-minded work are all for you. *Compatible signs:* Libra, Sagittarius, and other Aquarians. *Luck:* You tend to have good luck in raffles, draws, sweepstakes and lotteries. *Lucky number:* 4; *Day* – Friday; *Colours* – All variations in the Blue/Green range of shades; *Metal* – Uranium; *Gems* – Opal, Garnet, Emerald, Amethyst.

PISCES February 19—March 20. *Personality:* You are warm, sympathetic and sentimental. You are easy going, love to care for people and are inclined to be a day-dreamer. *Careers:* A wide variety of jobs seem suitable – try catering, nursing, welfare work; artistic careers in films, photography, advertising and publicity. *Compatible signs:* Scorpio, Capricorn, Cancer, Taurus, are all signs that can understand you. *Luck:* You have faith in such things as lucky mascots and charms which seem able to bring you luck. *Ruling planet:* Jupiter and Neptune, planets that help you to 'land on your feet'. *Lucky number:* 7; *Day* – Thursday; *Colours* – Misty shades of Green, Grey, Lovat, Heather, Turquoise, Aquamarine; *Metal* – Tin; *Gems* – Emerald, Garnet and Aquamarine.

Keeping Pets

Dogs

Choosing a dog for a pet needs careful thought. It isn't enough to decide, 'That's for me!' when a friendly puppy in a pet shop rolls his eyes at you and licks your hand. What you have to consider is the size he will reach, the amount of exercise he'll need, and the amount he is likely to eat. You also have to make up your mind whether the desire to have a dog is just a passing fancy or a feeling that will remain, for when you have bought or been given a dog not only does that dog belong to you, *but you belong to him*. Dogs have as intense a feeling of loyalty as do human beings, and an unwanted dog feels just as lost as an unwanted person does.

There are many breeds from which to choose a dog that suits your requirements; or you may prefer a mongrel to a pedigree pup. Your local dogs' home will be able to help you there. Remember that a large dog can be an encumbrance in a flat or a small house—and his food bills will be high. A dog bred for an active open-air life may be unhappy in a town. So think it over carefully before making your choice.

As soon as you get your dog, buy him a licence if he is over six months old. This can be obtained at any Post Office. It is against the law to keep a dog without a licence.

He will need a box or basket. Dog baskets are rather expensive, but a comfortable box can be made out of scrap wood without any difficult carpentry. Make it big enough for him to move about in and to stretch in his sleep, yet cosy enough to keep him warm. The box should be in a corner free from draughts, and should be lined with several newspapers to keep in the warmth. On top of these he should have an old rug or blanket, or, alternatively, an old eiderdown. Don't just give him a pillow; most dogs like to roll themselves up in their bedding, just as many of us do. The bedding should be taken out of doors and shaken every day or two and the newspaper changed at frequent intervals.

If you have a garden and your dog is able to get plenty of exercise in it, then one short walk every day should be all he needs. Except in country districts, this should preferably be on a lead.

He will probably be untrained when you first get him. Training needs patience, and if it seems to take a long time, remember that the training of a human baby takes far longer. It will help your puppy if you can start off with a regular routine of meals, walks and grooming.

At first, puppies need to be let out of doors every two or three hours during the day. A few messes indoors must be expected, and the dog which learns quickly is the one which is praised for attending to his needs out of doors rather than the one which is punished for making a mess in the hall.

Teach your dog to 'come to heel' when taken out of doors without a lead. A little perseverance should make him completely obedient to your orders. A disobedient dog is less to blame than his owner, for a dog naturally regards man as his master and disobeys only when that master no longer deserves respect. To earn that respect, you have to be absolutely consistent about discipline. If your dog is

Cocker spaniel puppy

Airedale terrier

punished or spoken to sharply for making a mess on the pavements then he must *always* be punished or spoken to sharply for it. If he is praised when he comes to heel promptly, then he must *always* be praised. Above all, he must never be punished without knowing why.

Grooming needs vary for different breeds of dogs. Short-haired dogs need only a brisk rub-down from time to time with a rough towel or a brush; long-haired varieties need more frequent attention, with a steel comb and stiff brush. Your dog should be taught to look forward to this as a regular habit and should be complimented on his smartness afterwards. Washing need not be frequent for most breeds and should be done either with ordinary toilet soap or with dog soap sold by your pet-shop. Don't use kitchen soap, as the soda will harm his coat as well as irritate the pores of his skin. The temperature of the water should be moderate. Immediately after his bath your dog should be very thoroughly dried, otherwise he'll undertake this himself and in doing so probably make himself dirtier than he was before.

A dog's diet should consist of about a half ounce of meat for each pound of his weight, as well as about the same amount of cereal and vegetable matter. The quantities required must be adjusted according to the amount of exercise the dog gets. It is as important not to over-feed as it is not to under-feed, as over-feeding brings about various stomach troubles which may be difficult to cure.

Meat should not be overcooked, and many dogs prefer it raw. Bones, carefully chosen in order to avoid those which may cause injury through sharp splinters, are used by most dogs more as playthings than as a source of food, and to compensate a dog for the lack of mineral from bones he should be given a small amount of ground bone-meal in his diet.

A puppy should be fed four or five times a day, but by the time a dog is fully grown he should be fed only one main meal a day and should know the exact time at which to expect his food. Your dog should always have access to a supply of fresh water.

Cats

A kitten is ready to leave its mother at eight weeks, by which time it should have learned to attend to its needs out of doors or in an ash-box placed in a corner. A cat needs the same kind of bedding as a dog, also the same chance to go out of doors for exercise. Do not attempt to

help a cat keep itself clean; unlike dogs, cats spend much of their time doing this very efficiently, and your assistance will not be appreciated.

Kittens should receive several feeds a day, but by the time they are six months old this should have been reduced to two, or even one, given at regular times of the day. A healthy adult cat should receive about half an ounce of food for every pound it weighs. Milk, meat, fish, liver, and most table scraps, providing they do not contain too much spice, are their basic diet. A cat should always have access to a supply of fresh water.

Mice

All varieties of tame mice need a warm temperature,

and must be given a cage with plenty of room. Its floor should be littered with clean sawdust, which should be changed frequently. Grain mixture and bread is the ideal diet, with fragments of cheese and greenstuff. The water supply must be kept fresh.

Hamsters

Golden hamsters are kept in the same way as mice. As well as bread and cereal, they enjoy carrots, maize meal and milk.

Guinea-pigs

Guinea-pigs are best kept out of doors in a warm shed which is thoroughly proofed against rats, cats and dogs. They should have an outdoor run on the sheltered side of their shed. The shed itself should contain plenty of litter for bedding; wood-wool or fine shavings are ideally suitable for this. The bedding should be changed frequently to avoid unpleasant smells and the danger of disease. Guinea-pigs need about an ounce of cereal daily (bran and crushed oats), with a plentiful supply of garden greenstuff. Fresh water should always be available.

Rabbits

Rabbits require much the same housing as guinea-pigs but the food may be more varied. Rabbits will thrive on many kinds of household scraps, such as bread, cooked potatoes and plenty of green food.

Tortoises

A tortoise, as he carries his own house with him, needs only a shelter to keep off heavy rain and wind. A small wooden box on its side in the garden is adequate. In a garden which contains plants of value it may be necessary to limit the tortoise's movements by boards or low fencing, for he will spend much of his time wandering about and sampling different kinds of greenstuff. In winter he will hibernate, and it is important to know *where*, as once this has happened he must not be disturbed until the warmer weather returns. If brought into a greenhouse or shed to hibernate in a box, he should be given plenty of straw and dry leaves with which to cover himself completely. If he hibernates in the garden, he will probably fail to cover himself with a thick enough layer of earth to keep out the frost, and so a thick wad of straw should be placed on top.

During the summer the moisture from greenstuff may be insufficient; a tortoise should then be given a supply of fresh water in a shallow plate or saucer.

Cage Birds

Canaries require a diet composed of canary seed, summer rape seed, cuttlefish bone and a little greenstuff. Fresh water should always be provided in the cage. Budgerigars should receive millet and canary seed, with lettuce or other greenstuff in small quantities. The secret of successful bird-keeping is attention to cleanliness; the cage must be kept spotlessly clean and the water changed as often as possible. Care must also be taken to prevent draughts.

79

Indoor Games

Indoor games can be excellent fun, especially as your skill in mastering them increases. Here are the rules of a few of the standard games:

Chess

The game is for two players, one taking the white players and the other the black. The board is of sixty-four squares, alternately black and white. At the beginning of the game each player has a white square in the right-hand corner nearest him. The lines of squares going from left to right are called *ranks,* those from top to bottom *files,* and the paths from corner to corner and those parallel to them are called *diagonals.*

Each player has sixteen pieces: a king (K), a queen (Q), two rooks (R) (or castles), two bishops (B), two knights (Kt) and eight pawns (P). At the beginning of the game the pieces are laid out as in the diagram. Note that the white queen occupies a white square, and the black queen opposite occupies a black square. White moves first. When games of chess are described each square has a number, or rather two, one with reference to the white pieces, and one to the black. These are shown in the second diagram. If in the first move of the game the pawn on the square QB2 (known as the queen's bishop pawn) is moved two squares forward the move will be written thus: 1. QBP — QB4.

The object of the game is to capture the opponent's king. Pieces capture an enemy piece by moving to the square occupied by that piece, the captured piece being removed from the board.

Pieces move as follows:

King : one square in any direction, either along a rank, a file or diagonally.

Queen :   any number of squares in any direction.

Rook :   any number of squares along a rank or file.

Bishop :   any number of squares diagonally. It follows that a bishop on a white square can only move to another white square.

Knight :   two squares along a rank or file and then one square to left or right. If you look at the diagram, the knight on QKt1 can make his first move to QR3, QB3 or Q2. A knight in the centre of the board will have eight possible squares to move to. A knight is the only piece on the board that may jump over other pieces.

Pawn :   A pawn on his first move may move either one or two squares along his file. Subsequently he may

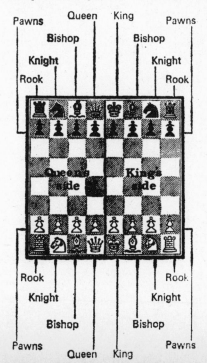

81

move only one square forward. Pawns, unlike other pieces may only move forwards towards the opponent's end of the board. If a pawn reaches the end of its file, it may be exchanged for another piece, usually, of course, the most powerful, the Queen. A player by this means may have two queens on the board. When capturing an opponent's piece, however, a pawn moves one square forward diagonally, either to left or right.

BLACK

QR1 QR8	QKt1 QKt8	QB1 QB8	Q1 Q8	K1 K8	KB1 KB8	KKt1 KKt8	KR1 KR8
QR2 QR7	QKt2 QKt7	QB2 QB7	Q2 Q7	K2 K7	KB2 KB7	KKt2 KKt7	KR2 KR7
QR3 QR6	QKt3 QKt6	QB3 QB6	Q3 Q6	K3 K6	KB3 KB6	KKt3 KKt6	KR3 KR6
QR4 QR5	QKt4 QKt5	QB4 QB5	Q4 Q5	K4 K5	KB4 KB5	KKt4 KKt5	KR4 KR5
QR5 QR4	QKt5 QKt4	QB5 QB4	Q5 Q4	K5 K4	KB5 KB4	KKt5 KKt4	KR5 KR4
QR6 QR3	QKt6 QKt3	QB6 QB3	Q6 Q3	K6 K3	KB6 KB3	KKt6 KKt3	KR6 KR3
QR7 QR2	QKt7 QKt2	QB7 QB2	Q7 Q2	K7 K2	KB7 KB2	KKt7 KKt2	KR7 KR2
QR8 QR1	QKt8 QKt1	QB8 QB1	Q8 Q1	K8 K1	KB8 KB1	KKt8 KKt1	KR8 KR1

WHITE

There are two other special moves. The first is the *en passant* move. As stated, a pawn may move on its first move two squares forward, but if by doing so it avoids capture by an opposing pawn (i.e. if by moving only one square forward an opposing pawn could have taken it), then the opposing player may capture the pawn *en passant,* and may take it as if it had moved only one square.

The second special move is known as "castling". If a player has not moved his king or the rook on his king's side, but the intervening squares are empty, he may castle by moving his king to KKt1 and his rook to KB1. This is known as castling on the king's side. Similarly, he may castle on the queen's side by moving his king to QB1 and his rook to Q1. A player may not castle if his king is in check (which will be explained later), nor may he castle more than once in a game.

How does a player win by capturing his opponent's king? First, the expression "check" must be explained. If a player has one or more of his pieces so positioned that he may capture his opponent's king on the next move, then that king is in check, and the attacking-player must announce "check". The opponent must then use his next move to avert the danger, which can be done by capturing the threatening piece, by moving one of his own pieces to an interposing square to block the threat, or by moving his king to a safe square. If none of these alternatives is open to him, then the king is "checkmated", and the game is lost.

A game can be drawn at any time by agreement. A game is also drawn if stalemate occurs, which is when a player can move only his king, which is not in check, but can move it only to a position of check. A draw by repetition can be claimed if a position repeats itself three times, or if a player can place his opponent's king in perpetual check: that is, if a player cannot checkmate but can check the opposing king on every move, he may claim a draw.

At the beginning of a game, a player should attempt to get

his more powerful pieces into play as quickly as possible. For example, if the pawn in front of the king is moved, diagonals are immediately opened up for the queen and a bishop. There are several recognized openings to chess games, each with a name, and there are recognized counters to them, all designed to achieve good positions early in the game. There are many books published on opening gambits, as they are called, as indeed there are on all stages of a chess game, and a beginner who wishes to play well should obtain and study one of the books designed for learners.

Draughts

This is played on the black squares of a chess-board, using two sets of men, each consisting of twelve black and twelve red or white circular pieces. These are arranged on the black squares of the first three rows at each end of the board, and move one square forward, diagonally. The purpose of the game is to capture all the opponent's pieces, which is done by jumping across them to a vacant square beyond. If, by so doing, the attacker then lands on a square from which it is able to capture again, it does so without waiting for the next move. On reaching the opponent's back line, a piece becomes a King by having a captured piece placed on top, and thenceforward may move forward or back.

A player in a position to make a capture must do so.

Backgammon

This game has had a great revival of interest in the 1970s. It is for two players. It is played with a special board, fifteen black and fifteen white counters or stones and two dice. The illustration shows the board set out at the beginning of the game. The board is divided by a bar into two halves; by arrangement one half is the inner table and one half the outer—in the illustration the left half is the inner. Projecting from each side of the board are twelve points of alternate colours (numbered in the illustration for convenience, but not numbered on the board itself). Each player rolls one die, and the higher plays first. The object is to move all fifteen stones into the inner table and thence off the board. The first player to bear off his stones is the winner. Each player moves towards his inner table (i.e. white moves clockwise in the illustration, black anti-clockwise).

The first player rolls both dice and may move his stones according to his score. He may move two stones, each according to the score of one die, or he may move the same stone twice. For instance, if White rolls 6—3, he may move one stone from Black's point 1 to point 10, or he may move one stone from Black 12 to White 7 and one from Black 12 to

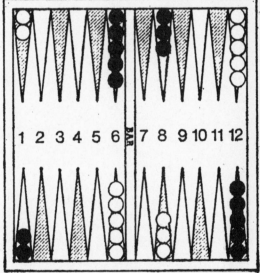

INNER TABLE   BLACK   OUTER TABLE

1 2 3 4 5 6   7 8 9 10 11 12

INNER TABLE   WHITE   OUTER TABLE

White 10. Doubles are scored twice over, for instance a double-6 would enable the player to move four stones each six points, or, if he prefers, two stones twelve points. A player must always move if possible. If he cannot move, he loses the turn. If he can move only the score on one die, he must, and if he can move the score on either die, but not both, he must take the higher score.

No point may be occupied by stones of opposite colours. If a player has two or more stones on a point, he has made the point, and the other player must not land on it. Thus if Whites first throw is 5-5, he cannot move either stone on Black's point 1, as the first 5 would take either to Black's point 6, which is already occupied by five Black stones. A single stone on a point is called a blot. If the opponent can move a stone to that point, the blot is hit and is removed from the board and placed on the bar in the centre of the board. When a player's stone is on the bar, he must enter it before he moves any other stone. A stone enters on the adverse inner table. Thus if Black has a stone on the bar, and White has two stones on each point of his own inner table, it is clear that Black cannot move, and must wait until a point is available before he can enter his stone.

A player's first task is to move all fifteen stones into his inner table. Once he has achieved this, he may begin to bear off his stones. A stone is borne off by throwing the number equivalent to the point occupied by the stone. Thus if White has all his stones in his inner table, and throws 4-2, he may bear off stones from points 4 and 2. Or, of course, he may bear off one stone from point, 6. Or, if he wishes, he may bear off a stone from point 2, and move a stone from point 6 to point 2. If, at this stage of the game, a player throws a number higher than his highest occupied point, he may bear off a stone from his highest occupied point. For example, if he throws a 6, and his highest occupied point is 5, he may bear off the stone on point 5.

It will be seen that backgammon is in effect a race, with

each player moving his stones in opposite directions round the board in an attempt to bear them all off first. A player should try to make points, which render his own stones safe for the time being and also impede his opponent's stones. It is impossible to avoid blots altogether, but it should be noted that if a blot is hit and placed on the bar it is easier to enter it early in the game than it might be later when an opponent may have made some of his inner table points.

Sketching and Painting

This is a hobby that can give anyone a great deal of enjoyment and satisfaction—even if he has always felt that he 'can't draw a straight line'. In fact, it is often those having the greatest doubts as to their ability who eventually produce the best results. Painting and drawing are wonderful ways of increasing your powers of observation, and they can provide a far more personal record of the things you see than the camera can ever hope to achieve.

For pencil sketching a beginner needs a range of soft and hard pencils, some sticks of soft charcoal, a block or book of cartridge paper, a soft india-rubber and a charcoal eraser. A small bottle of charcoal fixative, together with a blower, will be needed to 'fix' charcoal drawings.

Art classes at school may have taught the chief rule of perspective; briefly, it is that distant objects appear smaller. If you stand in the middle of a railway track and look along it, the two rails appear to draw closer together in the distance. This applies to all objects; the wall of a house, viewed at an angle, appears taller at the end nearest the point at which you are standing. Easy practice in perspective can be had by sketching open country with fields. Trees, hedges and fences will give you a challenge in perspective which will stand you in good stead when you tackle something more difficult.

Light and shade in pencil sketching are achieved by depth of pencil shading. There is no need to pay too much attention to the way in which this shading is applied, or to try to put in a great many details. The best way to begin is to look for the main masses of light and dark in front of you and to try to represent their shapes, as well as their sizes and tones

Drawing in perspective

level view

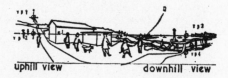

uphill view   downhill view

road dips   road humps

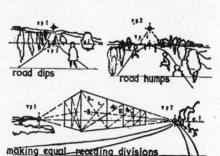

making equal receding divisions

V. P. = vanishing point
e.l. = eye level - of viewer
1,2,3,4,5,6,7. = order of construction lines

in relation to one another. The more outstanding details that you see can be put in later. You should, however, bear in mind that a sketch of a scene is always a simplification of that scene.

Should you wish to sketch in pen and ink—a more limiting medium for a beginner—you will need a harder-sufaced paper, a small range of nibs and a bottle of black India ink. You can also buy India ink in a variety of colours.

If you would like to try painting, you may choose to start with oil paints, water-colours, poster colours or even pastels. If you are beginning in oils, you will find prepared hardboard a satisfactory surface to use and inexpensive compared with canvas. It is best to equip yourself with large brushes, to use a good-sized surface, and to treat the subject matter broadly, looking for areas of colours and tones, and for their relations to one another. Try some exercises which will help you to see how one colour affects another; place patches of different colours, or of different shades of one colour, next to each other and study the effect. Some colours are heavier than others; some come forward while others seem to recede; some combinations of colours are harmonious while some are discordant. All of these discoveries can be applied to your painting. Many other colour exercises can be found in the various books on painting which are in your public library.

You may find it useful to keep to a fairly small selection of colours at first. The following is a suggested basic palette for oil painting:

Cadmium Yellow	Ultramarine (blue)
Cadmium Red	Viridian (green)
Alizarin Crimson	Flake, Titanium or Zinc White
Monastral Blue	Ivory Black

Useful colours to add to this are Yellow Ochre, Light Red, Cobalt Blue and Terre Verte (earth green).

Bookbinding

Whole works have been written on the *proper* way to set about binding books at home, but the methods described require a heavy press. This simple way of putting sturdy covers on paper-backed books needs nothing except scraps of material, cardboard, scissors, glue and common sense.

First find a piece of stiff material big enough to cover the book with an inch to spare all round. If no stiff material is handy, use a piece of an old sheet, well starched. Cut out three pieces of cardboard, the sizes of the front, back and spine of the book. Glue these to the material as in the diagram.

Now cut slots at A, bend the material down and glue on to the card. Next glue B to the front and back of the book. Fold down and glue the edges of the material, being careful to make neat, flat folds at the corners. Finally, paste white paper on the inside of each cover, to hide the folds of the material. If you want the title of the book on the spine, neat lettering on a strip of white paper glued into place will finish off a thoroughly professional-looking job.

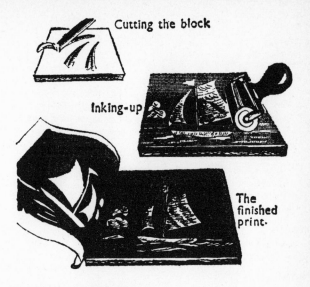

Cutting the block

Inking-up

The finished print.

Printing from Linocuts

You can make black-and-white pictures or full-colour illustrations for Christmas cards and other purposes by linocut printing. A piece of high-quality thick lino is needed. This can be bought ready cut from an art materials shop in sizes from 3 × 3 inches upwards, or can be trimmed from scraps after laying household lino. Thin lino isn't suitable, as the design for printing has to be cut into its surface. The lino should have a plain surface without any glossy design on it.

On the lino, draw the outlines of the picture which is to be made, remembering that the final result will be the exact reverse of your drawing. Avoid excessive detail; a picture drawn with a few bold strokes of the pencil is most likely to be successful. The outline should then be gone over with black India ink so that it will not be rubbed away by your hand while cutting the outlines.

You may already have a narrow 'V'-shaped chisel suitable for gouging out the unwanted areas of lino, but if not, one can be quite easily made from the broken rib of an old umbrella, fixed into a wooden handle and then ground to a sharp cutting edge. When all the areas which are not to be printed have been chiselled away, the picture is ready for inking.

This is done by means of a small roller and a piece of glass. The roller should be made of gelatine compound, and small ones can be obtained very cheaply at any art materials shop. So can small tubes of printing ink, and suitable paper.

Squeeze a small amount of printing ink on to the sheet of glass and work it to a thin, even surface with the roller which, of course, will then be similarly coated. Roll back and forth across the linocut; then place a sheet of printing paper on the linocut and press evenly and gently over the surface. This is best done with a circle of wood such as five-ply, of about four inches in diameter. This can easily be made with a fret-saw. The under side, which is to be used for pressing and rubbing, should have its edge smoothed off to prevent it from digging into the surface of the paper. Care should be taken that the lino does not slip while on the paper.

Linocuts in more than one colour can be made in the same way. A block is made for each colour of the full picture, and the only extra problem is that of making sure that all blocks 'register' accurately—in other words, that the colours do not overlap where this is not intended. If the picture is first drawn on to tracing paper and the appropriate outlines are then transferred on to each block of lino, this problem should not arise.

FIRST AID WHEN OUT AND ABOUT

When giving First Aid remember that unless you've had training through the Red Cross or some similar organisation you may do more harm by doing too much than too little. Your attempts to treat serious burns or to straighten a fracture may make it more difficult for the doctor who later has to cure the patient.

The *first* object of First Aid is to save life: that is, to prevent the casualty from dying before medical aid can be obtained. Therefore, look immediately for signs of asphyxia or severe bleeding and, if necessary, stop bleeding and begin artificial respiration. *Every second counts.*

The *second* object is to prevent any deterioration in the condition of the casualty. This is achieved by attending to the injuries which the casualty has sustained, and preventing further injury.

Never attempt to give an unconscious person anything to drink.

ASPHYXIA

Asphyxia is a condition whereby air is prevented from entering the lungs of the body such as by Suffocation, Drowning, Gas, Choking and Strangulation.

Asphyxia can also occur in cases of electric shock.

If the casualty has stopped breathing do not lose an instant, act quickly and methodically.

1. Clear away any obstruction round the neck or face, or within the mouth or throat.
2. Lay the casualty on his back and kneel beside his head.
3. Place one hand under his neck and the other hand on top of his head.
4. Lift the neck and tilt the head backwards as far as possible; this may clear the airway and the casualty may begin to breathe. If he does not, immediately commence artifical respiration.

ARTIFICIAL RESPIRATION

Mouth to Mouth Method

1. Keep the head tilted well backwards.
2. With one hand pinch the patient's nose shut and keep his head bent back. With the other hold his chin to keep his mouth open (but do not let fingers get in the way of the mouth or press on the neck).
3. Open your mouth wide, seal the casualty's mouth with your own and blow in smoothly.
4. Watch out of the corner of your eye, if possible, for the rise of the chest. Now remove your mouth to allow the air out again and the chest to fall. At the same time you take another breath in.
5. Repeat 3 and 4 as soon as his chest has fallen; for a baby or small child blow gently and carefully. In no circumstances blow violently into a baby's lungs.

Points to bear in mind:

Are your lips fully sealed right round the patient's mouth?

Is the nose properly pinched shut low down?

Is the jaw pushed forward with the mouth open?

Are the back of the throat and windpipe clear?

Are you still keeping the head bent back as far as possible?

Breathe into the patient firmly and fully

Lift your mouth off and let the patient's chest empty naturally

Revised Holger Nielsen Method

1. Lay casualty face down with head turned to one side, arms above his head with elbows bent so that the upper part of the cheek is resting on his hands and his mouth clear of the ground.
2. Kneel at his head, placing one knee near casualty's head and one foot alongside his elbow.
3. Place your hands over casualty's shoulder blades, with thumbs touching in the mid-line and fingers spread out, the arms being kept straight.
4. Rock forward gently with arms straight and let pressure be applied by weight of upper part of body only (see Fig. 1).
5. Rock back with arms straight, as you slide your hands to just below the elbows of casualty (see Fig. 2).
6. Continue to rock back so lifting casualty's arms until tension is felt (see Fig. 3), to cause inhalation.
7. Then lower casualty's arms down and place your hands on his back as in Fig. 1.
8. Repeat the above movement with rhythmic rocking at the rate of 12 times a minute, until breathing has been re-established.
9. If the arms are injured, place them by the sides of the body then do the complete procedure, but insert your hands under the casualty's shoulders and raise them for inhalation.

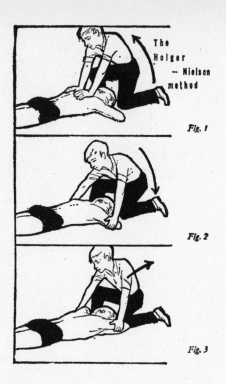

The Holger — Nielsen method

Fig. 1

Fig. 2

Fig. 3

DROWNING

Do not lose an instant; act quickly and methodically.

1. Quickly clear mouth of any false teeth, weeds, or obvious obstruction.
2. Give mouth to mouth artificial respiration as described on previous page.

3. Maintain body heat of patient by placing rug or coat over and under him and continue artificial respiration until a doctor has pronounced the patient dead.
4. When consciousness returns, keep casualty lying down in recovery position and treat for shock (on next page).

ELECTRIC SHOCK

Act promptly, taking care not to electrocute yourself.
1. Switch off current if possible or unplug cable.
2. If this is not possible stand on an insulating material (a dry rubber mackintosh, or piece of wood) and pull casualty away by means of rope or walking stick, but not an umbrella which has metal ribs. If possible avoid contact with the casualty's armpits.
3. Apply Mouth to Mouth Resuscitation if breathing has stopped. Beware of fractures and burnt areas.

Note: Very high-powered currents (pylon wires, power stations) can be very dangerous if approached: keep clear and do not attempt rescue until current is known to have been cut off.

BLEEDING OR HAEMORRHAGE

Mild bleeding

Act immediately.
Treat it as a wound (page 102): firm bandage pressure will cope with it.

Severe bleeding (fast and dangerous)

With fingers and thumb press the wound edges firmly together. Keep this pressure at least ten minutes to let a clot form. Raise a bleeding arm or leg (but not if it could be fractured). Replace your finger pressure by that of a firm dressing pad and bandage as soon as you can. Keep the

How to protect oneself from lightning
If there is no shelter available, keep away from

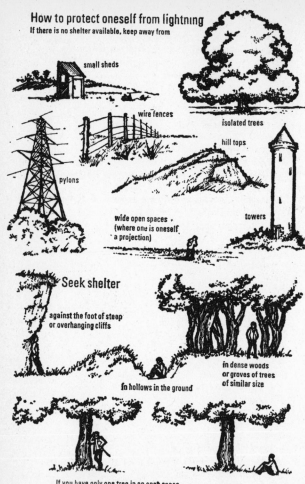

small sheds

isolated trees

wire fences

hill tops

pylons

towers

wide open spaces
(where one is oneself
a projection)

Seek shelter

against the foot of steep
or overhanging cliffs

in dense woods
or groves of trees
of similar size

in hollows in the ground

If you have only one tree in an open space
DO NOT lean against it but keep several feet away and do not touch it

injured part at rest. If blood continues to ooze through the bandage leave the bandage on and add more padding and firm bandaging over it.

SHOCK PREVENTION

In any serious injury:
1. Stop any bleeding.
2. Lay casualty on his back with head to one side and legs slightly raised, unless they are fractured.
3. Loosen clothing at neck and waist.
4. Maintain body heat of casualty by placing rug or coat around casualty. Do not give anything to drink or apply hot water bottles.
5. Handle as gently as possible and avoid any unnecessary movements.
6. See there is plenty of fresh air, and protect against any inclemency of weather.
7. Be cheerful and encouraging.
8. Get a doctor as soon as possible.

FAINTING

1. If the casualty feels faint, sit him down and lower his head between the knees.
2. Loosen clothing at neck and waist.
3. Allow plenty of fresh air, but protect from cold.
4. When casualty regains strength gradually raise him and give sips of water, tea or coffee.
5. If he becomes unconscious, act as below.

UNCONSCIOUSNESS: THE RECOVERY POSITION

1. Examine the casualty to see that:
   (a) He is breathing — If not apply artificial respiration (see page 94).

(b) He is not bleeding — If he is give appropriate treatment.

2. If you suspect fractures which would prevent moving him, turn the head to one side and ensure a clear airway by tilting the head slightly backwards.

3. If he can be moved, put him into the Recovery Position; turn patient on to side; the lower leg and arm are stretched out behind him. The upper arm and leg should be bent so that the hip and elbow joints are at about a right angle. The head should be tilted slightly backwards

4. Do not give patient anything to drink.

BURNS AND SCALDS

Never handle a burned area and do not apply any lotions or ointment. The object of treatment of burns is to reduce the heat of the burn.

1. Place the burned area in cool clean water for at least ten minutes and until pain is relieved.

2. Apply a clean dry dressing.

3. Arrange for transport to hospital as soon as possible. The transport of a seriously burned patient to hospital should not be delayed.

4. Burn blisters should not be pricked.

5. Reassure the casualty, as this is most important to his recovery. Guard against shock (page 99).

FRACTURES

Do not move casualty until injured part is immobilised, unless life is in immediate danger from surrounding environment, i.e. falling buildings, fire etc.

Closed (Bone not exposed)

1. Ensure casualty is in comfortable condition.

2. Keep warm, handle gently and generally guard against shock (see page 99).

The Recovery Position
Lying on one side.
Head bent back; face bent down.
Upper arm bent at right angle to shoulder
and elbow; upper hand near the face.
Upper leg bent at right angle at hip and knee.
Lower arm and leg stretched out behind.

3. Immobilise injured part by means of bandages and slings. The chest wall or the sound leg serve as good splints. In certain circumstances well padded splints may be required.
   (a) In the case of an arm, apply padding; bandage and support arm in a sling with the elbow bent and hand pointing to uninjured shoulder. If elbow itself is fractured, keep arm straight.
   (b) If a leg, pad well between the knees and ankles; bandage the sound leg to the injured one.
4. Never try to set the bones.
5. Do not give food or drink, as anaesthetic may have to be given shortly.

Get a doctor or send to hospital quickly.

Open (Wound exposes Bone)

Treat as for a simple fracture but, in addition:
1. Cover the wound with a dry dressing.
2. Stop any bleeding (see pages 97).
3. Especially take care to counteract shock.

Note : Do not try to push protruding bone back into place.

DISLOCATIONS

1. Support the limb in the most comfortable position. Use plenty of padding with bandages. Never attempt to reduce a dislocation.
2. Reasssure the casualty which will help to control shock.
3. Guard against shock (see page 99).
4. In cases of the lower jaw, remove any dentures if possible and support the jaw by a bandage tied over the top of the head.
5. Transfer patient to hospital.

SPRAINS AND STRAINS

1. Immobilise injured part.
2. Apply cold compress where possible.
3. Do not remove shoe or boot, unless swelling of the foot is great.
4. Arrange for transport to hospital.
5. If there is any doubt as to the extent of the injury treat as a fracture.

POISONING

Poisons fall into two categories.
(a) Those poisons which burn.
(b) Those which do not burn.

Unconscious Casualty

1. Ensure he is breathing freely; place him in the Recovery Position.
2. Should he not be breathing commence artificial respiration at once.
3. Tranfer to hospital immediately.

Conscious Casualty

1. Ask the casualty exactly what happened.
2. (a) If there are no stains on the lips or mouth (indicating burning), make him vomit, by giving him to drink 2 tablespoons of salt to a glass of water. Repeat this once.
   (b) If there are stains, DO NOT make him vomit, but dilute the poison by giving slow drinks of water, milk or barley water.
3. Transfer casualty to hospital at once without delay.
Note : In all cases of poisoning any bottles or other containers found must be sent with the casualty to hospital.

SNAKE BITES

Generally speaking the only poisonous snake to be found in the wild state in Great Britain is the Adder, which is characteristically recognised by zig-zag lines on the snake's back.

1. It is very important to reassure the patient.
2. Lay the casualty down at absolute rest.
3. Put a clean dry dressing over the point.
4. Splint the affected limb as for a fracture.
5. Transport the casualty to hospital as a stretcher case.

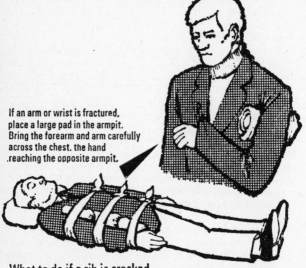

If an arm or wrist is fractured, place a large pad in the armpit. Bring the forearm and arm carefully across the chest, the hand reaching the opposite armpit.

What to do if a rib is cracked

Padding between the limb and the body. Broad bandages should be placed round the upper arm and the body, just below the elbow and the body, and round the wrist and thigh.

Anatomy

Like big buildings the body is constructed round a framework of girders. To this frame or skeleton all the muscles and important organs are attached.

The backbone (spine) is made up of ring-like bones, and down the middle runs the spinal cord. At the top of the spine is the head, which is like a bone box protecting the brain.

Attached to the spine is a cage of bones, the ribs, which protect the heart, lungs and liver. These ribs are joined at the front to the breast-bone.

To this breast-bone are joined the two collar-bones, and to these the two shoulder-blades and to these the arms.

At the lower end of the spine is the pelvis, to which are attached the legs.

The upper arms and thighs have one bone each; the forearms and lower legs, two bones each. The wrists and ankles contain groups of small square bones. Longer ones are in the palms and soles of the feet, and not quite such long ones in the fingers and toes.

There are seven major organs which carry out the various functions of the body.

The brain directs the body's working by receiving messages through the nervous system and by sending messages to other parts of the body along the spinal cord and nerves.

The heart pumps the blood through the body by way of the arteries, and receives it back through the veins.

The lungs take air into the body by means of the upper respiratory tract. They also expel carbon dioxide, a waste product taken from the blood.

The stomach takes in food, begins the digestive process and sends the food through the intestines to complete digestion.

The liver and the pancreas discharge juices into the small intestine which aid in the digestion of food. The liver also stores vitamins, and aids in purifying the blood, while the pancreas regulates the amount of sugar in the blood.

The kidneys remove waste materials from the blood. These waste materials are carried to the bladder, where they are kept until evacuated from the body.

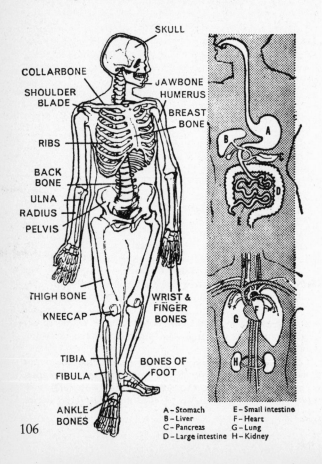

A – Stomach   E – Small intestine
B – Liver   F – Heart
C – Pancreas   G – Lung
D – Large intestine   H – Kidney

SKULL
COLLARBONE
JAWBONE
HUMERUS
SHOULDER BLADE
BREAST BONE
RIBS
BACK BONE
ULNA
RADIUS
PELVIS
THIGH BONE
WRIST & FINGER BONES
KNEECAP
TIBIA
FIBULA
BONES OF FOOT
ANKLE BONES

Collecting as a Hobby

Collecting Old Books

This is a hobby for those who enjoy reading and who are, perhaps, interested in writing as well. And though buying new books is expensive, collecting old ones is a hobby that, if carried out carefully, need cost no more than a few pence a week.

Your own interests and other hobbies will help you to decide the subjects which will form the basis of your collection. There are, of course, hundreds to choose from, but a few which can make absorbingly interesting collections without much cost are:

Printing—its history and development
Your favourite sport
What towns and countries looked like in the past
Early cars and railways
Wild life at home and abroad

These suggestions have been made bearing in mind the available sources of old books—second-hand book shops, junk shops and auction rooms. Very often at small auctions you can buy odd lots of books fifty or a hundred years old for prices as low as fifty pence for a hundred. Of this hundred, ninety-five are likely to be completely useless to you, but exchanges with other collectors, or even subsequent auctions, will enable you to get rid of the ones you don't want.

Condition is important if you are collecting books for their own sake, but if you are simply hoping, for instance, to accumulate pictures and information about early railways, you will not be unduly worried if some of your books have torn covers and missing pages. Damaged books can be repaired quite easily (see *Bookbinding,* page 90) so your bookcases need not remain untidy simply because your books, when you bought them, were in shabby condition.

Coin Collecting

This is a hobby in which the lucky collector can still come across rare finds of great value or tremendous historical interest. Unlike stamps and match-box labels, coins can be lost for centuries and still survive undamaged, and it is not unusual, when new ground is being turned over or old buildings are being demolished, for coins dating back even as far as Roman times to be unearthed. Coins have been in existence since about 700 B.C., and appeared in Britain before the last century B.C.

Modern coins of many countries can be obtained easily through exchange or by buying a bag of assorted foreign coins.

A cabinet to house your collection needs shallow drawers lined with baize into which holes have been cut to let the coins lie snugly without moving. A small gummed identification label can be stuck below each coin.

Collecting Match-box Labels

Collecting match-box labels, like stamp collecting, is a hobby dating back to the last century. You set about it by saving all you can find and making exchanges with other collectors for the ones you need.

Remove the labels from the boxes by soaking them for a few minutes in hot water, peeling them off, and then drying them between sheets of blotting paper. Loose-leaf albums are the best for mounting collections, and stamp-hinges will safely fix them to the page.

British match-box labels are usually rather dull and uninteresting in design, but there are thousands of foreign ones with highly-coloured action pictures on them. You can find labels showing portraits of native warriors, ships and planes, railways, and you can find some with exciting forgeries printed by wartime resistance groups, bearing slogans encouraging the guerrilla fighters.

Cheese-label Collecting

The proper name for this is 'fromology', and the makers of cheese in many countries have recognised the rapid growth of the hobby in recent years by issuing many new and colourful designs. It is possible to build up a collection of more than thirty thousand different labels by exchanging with other collectors. The original source of supply is, of course, your own family kitchen. Friends travelling abroad and pen pals in foreign countries can help to enlarge your collection.

A collection of cheese labels is best mounted and stored in the same way as a stamp collection, using stamp-hinges to fasten the labels in place in a safe way so that they can be removed for exchange or remounting without damage. Removing labels which are gummed tightly to the wrapping of the cheese is best done without using water, as certain labels have colours which 'run' when moistened. Suitable methods are levering the label off the paper by cautious work with a paper knife or peeling off one corner and allowing steam from a kettle to penetrate the glue without coming into direct contact with the printed surface.

There are plenty of different pictorial subjects on cheese labels, ranging from wild animals, flowers and country scenes to aircraft, ships and sportsmen.

NATURAL HISTORY

Facts and Figures in the Living World

The Animal Kingdom

Largest: the largest living animal is the Blue Whale (*Balaenoptera musculus*). This marine mammal can grow to a length of over 33 metres, and to a weight of more than 130 tonnes. Minute, shrimp-like creatures known as krill make up its entire diet. The largest living land animal is the African Elephant (*Loxodonta africanus*); this mammal has been recorded at a height of almost 4 metres, and with a weight of nearly 11 tonnes.

Smallest: it is impossible to distinguish between the animal and plant kingdoms when the smallest living organisms are concerned. Bacteria are minute, and some viruses are even smaller – all are far too small to be seen without microscopes.

Longest: the Atlantic Jellyfish *Cyanea arctica* has trailing tentacles which may be as long as 36 metres. The dome-like part of the body (known as the bell) may be over 2 metres in diameter.

Tallest: the Giraffe (*Giraffa camelopardalis*), found in parts of Africa, may measure 6 metres from the ground to the tips of its horns.

Fastest: the fastest animal is the spine-tailed Swift (*Chaetura caudacuta*). This bird can fly at well over 170 kilometres per hour. On land, the Cheetah (*Acinonyx jubata*), and the Prong-horned Antelope (*Antilocarpa americana*) of North America, can both reach speeds of 100 kilometres per hour.

Rarest: the shrew-like Tenrec *Dasogale fontoyonti* from Madagascar is probably the claimant to this title. Only one specimen has ever been found. (The commonest organisms are bacteria. They make up three-quarters of all living things.)

Strangest: the animal kingdom is full of strange and exotic creatures, and we have chosen a class of animals which rank among the most curious. They belong to a group of mammals called monotremes. They are the primitive egg-laying mammals, and they share features in common with both the reptiles and the mammals. The Platypus (*Ornithorhynchus anatinus*) inhabits the fresh waters of Australia and Tasmania. The soft, duckbilled snout is used for finding worms. It swims with the aid of its webbed feet and flattened tail. The Spiny Anteaters (*Tachyglossus* from Australia, and *Zaglossus* from New Guinea) have a long snout and a sticky tongue for feeding on worms and ants which they extract from burrows. Also, unlike any other mammals, all monotremes have spurs on their hind legs armed with venom.

Most poisonous: the most poisonous, or venomous, animal is a north Australian jellyfish known as the sea wasp (*Chironex fleckeri*). It has been estimated that its poison is more than 350 times more potent than that of the Portuguese Man o' war. The poison acts so quickly – death usually occurs only a few minutes after being stung – that there is usually no chance to attempt treatment.

The most venomous land animal is the Funnelweb Spider (*Atrax robustus*), a large south Australian species. No really effective treatment has been found for its venom, which is far more potent than that of even the most deadly snake.

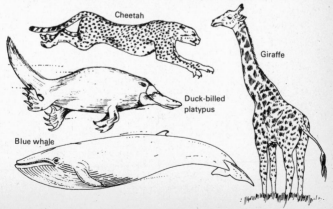

Cheetah

Giraffe

Duck-billed platypus

Blue whale

The Plant Kingdom

Largest: the Californian Redwood (*Sequoia gigantea*), an ever-green tree in the Sequoia National Park, grows to a height of 83 metres. At one place its girth is over 24 metres. Its weight is estimated to be over 2000 tonnes.

Tallest: the Coast Redwood (*Sequoia sempervirens*) of Oregon and California can grow to a height of 112 metres. Britain's tallest tree is the Grand Fir (*Abies grandis*) which stands 56 metres high.

Rarest: it is difficult to estimate the world's rarest plant, since many species are only known from one location, and some plants may not yet have been discovered. Among Britain's rarest are the Adder's Tongue Spearwort (*Ranunculus ophiglossifolius*), and the Coral Orchid *Epipogium aphyllum*.

Commonest: the world's commonest (in other words most widely distributed) plant is a grass known by its scientific name of *Cynodon dactylon*. It is found in South Africa, South America, Canada, New Zealand and Japan.

Deepest roots: the roots of a fig tree in South Africa are reputed to have penetrated the soil to a depth of 120 metres.

Oldest living: the oldest living tree is a Bristlecone Pine (*Pinus longaeva*) growing high up in Wheeler Park, California. It was found to be nearly 5,000 years old.

Strangest: the most bizarre group of plants must surely be the carnivorous, insectivorous plants. Of these, the Venus Fly

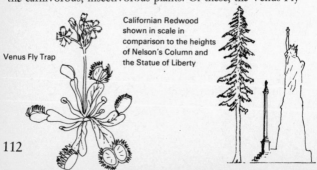

Venus Fly Trap

Californian Redwood shown in scale in comparison to the heights of Nelson's Column and the Statue of Liberty

Trap .(*Dionaea muscipula*) of North America is considered by many to be the most unusual. The Venus Fly Trap lives in soil lacking in nitrogen, so it obtains nitrogen from the bodies of flies and other small insects that it catches. The leaves have special traps on their ends and, when an insect lands on a trap, it snaps shut. The plant then digests the insect.

Facts and Figures in the World of the Past

The Animal Kingdom

Largest: *Brachiosaurus,* the Arm Lizard, is the largest land creature ever known to have lived. Bones have been found which indicate a specimen with a weight of over 100 tonnes. This reptilian dinosaur lived in the swamplands of the Mesozoic Era, over 150 million years ago. From the ground to its head it measured over 13 metres, and was 26 metres long from head to tail. Despite its enormous size, *Brachiosaurus* was a vegetarian, feeding on the plant growth it found around its swampland home. The largest carnivore (meat eater) ever known is *Tyrannosaurus,* the Tyrant Lizard, a fearsome dinosaur with massive jaws armed with rows of pointed teeth. *Tyrannosaurus* was 13 metres long and stood over 5 metres tall.

Longest: the longest known land animal was the dinosaur *Diplodocus,* which attained a length of 27 metres. It is possible that some extinct marine animals, such as the early forms of whale, exceeded this length, however.

The Plant Kingdom

Earliest forms of life: fossil evidence shows that simple forms of plant life existed over 3,000 million years ago.

Earliest flowering plant: the earliest fossil flower is a palm-like plant over 65 million years old, found in North America.

Classification

Classification is the method of grouping together organisms which have features in common. It also allows us to study the relationships that exist between one group and another. Within large groups of organisms with many common features, smaller groups are arranged with fewer features in common with each other. Usually systems of classification are arranged with the most primitive, or lowly, groups of animals or plants placed first, leading up to the most advanced. A few minor groups, and most extinct groups, have been excluded from the lists here.

Classification of the Animal Kingdom

Subkingdom Protozoa: single-celled animals.

Phylum Protozoa: microscopic, single-celled animals. *Subphylum Sarcomastigophora:* amoebas and flagellates. *Subphylum Sporozoa:* parasitic protozoans. *Subphylum Cnidospora:* parasitic protozoans with filamentous capsules on their spores (spores are resting stages in the life cycle). *Subphylum Ciliophora:* forms with hair-like cilia used for locomotion or feeding.

Subkingdom Metazoa: many-celled animals.

Phylum Porifera: sponges; the most lowly of the many celled animals; all are aquatic.

Phylum Cnidaria: mainly flower-like animals with bodies composed of two cell layers separated by a jelly-like layer called the mesoglea; food is usually captured by means of stinging tentacles. *Class Hydrozoa:* sea firs; also includes the Portuguese

114

Man-o'-war. *Class Scyphozoa:* the jellyfishes; mainly free-swimming, bell-shaped creatures. *Class Anthozoa:* sea-anemones and corals (corals secrete a stony covering in which the anemone-like creature lives).

Phylum Ctenophora: comb jellies; variously shaped animals with cilia which beat to drive the animal along.

Phylum Platyhelminthes: flatworms; leaf-like worms. *Class Turbellaria:* free-living worms found in water. *Class Trematoda:* the flukes; parasitic animals with complex life-cycles. *Class Cestoda:* tapeworms.

Phylum Nemertina: ribbon worms; often extremely long worms, usually found on the seashore.

Phylum Nemertoda: roundworms; free-living and parasitic types (e.g. hookworms) are found.

Phylum Brachiopoda: lamp shells; small animals attached to seabed by a stalk, and enclosed in a two-valved shell.

Phylum Annelida: segmented worms; a large phylum consisting of worms with a true body cavity (the coelom). *Class Polychaeta:* bristle worms; marine worms with well-defined heads; includes ragworms, lugworms and tube-dwelling worms. *Class Oligochaeta:* earthworms; mainly terrestrial or freshwater worms with a reduced head. *Class Hirudinea;* leeches; blood-sucking parasitic worms that attach themselves to their victim by suckers.

Phylum Mollusca: snails, slugs, bivalves and octopuses; many forms are covered in a hard shell, secreted by an outer body layer called the mantle; many fossils are known. *Class Monoplacophora:* simplest shelled molluscs. *Class Amphineura:* chitons; shell usually in eight parts. *Class Gastropoda:* slugs, snails and limpets; the shell is in one piece or, as in slugs, absent. *Class Bivalvia:* mussels, oysters; the shell is in two parts, hinged together. *Class Scaphopoda:* the tusk shells. *Class Cephalopoda:* squids and octopuses; most highly developed molluscs with powerful eyes, large 'brains' and tentacles for food capture.

Phylum Arthropoda: joint-legged animals; a huge phylum containing over 80 per cent of the entire animal kingdom; the body organs are contained within a hard exoskeleton. *Class Onychophora:* possible links between the worms and the arthropods. *Class Trilobita:* extinct clawed marine animals. *Class Merostomata:* king crabs. *Class Pycnogonida:* sea-spiders. *Class Arachnida:* spiders, scorpions, ticks and mites; 8-legged animals with the body divided into 2 parts. *Class Crustacea:* crabs, shrimps, lobsters, barnacles and woodlice. *Class Insecta:* insects; 3 pairs of legs and 2 pairs of wings are usually present; body divided into 3 parts; three-quarters of all animals are insects.

Phylum Ectoprocta: moss animals; tiny aquatic animals living in tubes, the whole mass together resembling seaweed.

Phylum Echinodermata: marine animals having bodies built on a 5-rayed plan; movement is by means of the water vascular system, a curious arrangement of water-filled canals which operate the tube feet. *Class Crinoidea:* feather-stars and sea-lilies; 5 pairs of arms; usually attached to the bottom. *Class Asteroidea:* starfishes. *Class Ophiuroidea:* brittle-stars; possess long, spiny arms. *Class Echinoidea:* sea-urchins, heart-urchins and sand-dollars; spherical creatures with long spines extending from the skin. *Class Holothuroidea:* sea-cucumbers; cucumber or worm-shaped creatures with a ring of tentacles surrounding the mouth.

Phylum Chaetognatha: arrow-worms; tiny, dart-like animals.

Phylum Hemichordata: worm-like animals whose body is divided into proboscis, collar and trunk.

Phylum Chordata: important phylum which includes the vertebrates, such as man; all chordates possess a hollow, dorsal nerve cord.

Subphylum Urochordata: salps; barrel-shaped animals.

Subphylum Cephalochordata: lancelets; small, burrowing, fish-like creatures.

Subphylum Vertebrata: vertebrates; the most advanced of all animals; vertebrates possess a brain-case, well-developed sense organs, a backbone of many separate bones (vertebrae) and usually paired limbs.

Class Agnatha: jawless fishes (hagfishes and lampreys).

Class Chondrichthyes: fishes with cartilaginous skeletons (sharks, skates and rays).

Class Osteichthyes: fishes with bony skeletons.

Class Amphibia: air-breathing land vertebrates which return to water to lay and fertilise their eggs. *Order Apoda:* limbless, burrowing forms. *Order Urodela:* newts and salamanders. *Order Anura:* frogs and toads.

Class Reptilia: cold-blooded vertebrates whose skin is usually covered in scales; eggs are fertilised inside the female and are usually laid within a protective shell. *Order Chelonia:* turtles and tortoises. *Order Rhynchocephalia:* tuatara lizard. *Order Crocodilia:* crododiles, caimans and alligators. *Order Squamata:* lizards and snakes.

The class Reptilia also includes some very important groups

of extinct animals. Among these are the marine Ichthyosaurs, the flying Pterosaurs, the mammal-like reptiles and the Saurischians and Ornithischians – these last two groups comprised the Dinosaurs.

Class Aves: birds; warm-blooded vertebrates with bodies covered with feathers; most birds can fly – all have the front limbs modified for wings. *Order Impennes:* penguins. *Order Struthioniformes:* ostriches. *Order Casuariiformes:* emus and cassowaries. *Order Apterygiformes:* moas and kiwis. *Order Rheiformes:* rheas. *Order Tinamiformes:* tinamous. *Order Gaviformes:* loons and divers. *Order Procellariiformes:* albatrosses, petrels and shearwaters. *Order Pelecaniformes:* pelicans and cormorants. *Order Ciconiiformes:* herons and bitterns. *Order Anseriformes:* ducks, geese and swans. *Order Falconiformes:* vultures, hawks, eagles, ospreys and falcons. *Order Columbiformes:* pigeons and doves. *Order Caprimulgiformes:* nightjars. *Order Coraciiformes:* kingfishers, toucans and woodpeckers. *Order Colymbiformes:* grebes. *Order Galliformes:* grouse and pheasants. *Order Gruiformes:* coots, rails and cranes. *Order Charadriiformes:* waders and gulls. *Order Psittaciformes:* parrots and macaws. *Order Cuculiformes:* cuckoos and road-runners. *Order Strigiformes:* owls. *Order Apodiformes:* swifts and hummingbirds. *Order Trogoniformes:* trogons. *Order Passeriformes:* perching birds; the largest order of birds containing many species such as the larks, swallows, crows, tits, wrens, thrushes, robins, warblers, flycatchers, starlings, finches and buntings.

Class Mammalia: mammals; warm-blooded creatures whose bodies are usually covered with hair; young develop inside the mother, except in primitive forms; young are suckled. *Subclass Prototheria, Order Monotremata:* egg-laying mammals; platypus and spiny ant-eaters. *Subclass Metatheria, Order Marsupalia:* primitive mammals in which the young develop in a pouch called the marsupium; marsupials are found in Australasia and parts of South America; wombats, wallabies, kangaroos, bandicoots and phalangers. *Subclass Eutheria:* the most advanced mammals; the young develop inside a special internal structure called the placenta. *Order Insectivora:* moles, flying lemurs, hedgehogs and shrews. *Order Chiroptera:* bats. *Order Primata:* monkeys, apes, lemurs, lorises and man. *Order Edentata:* sloths, armadillos and ant-eaters. *Order Pholidota:* pangolins. *Order Rodenta:* rats, mice, hamsters, squirrels, beavers, guinea pigs and porcupines. *Order Lagomorpha:* hares and rabbits. *Order Carnivora:* includes the Feloidea (mongoose, hyena, lynx, bobcats, tigers, lion and cheetah); the Canoidea (stoats, weasels, wolves, foxes, jackals, pandas, racoons and bears); the Phocoidea (seals) and the Otaroidea (walrus, furseals and sealions). *Order Cetacea:* whales, dolphins and porpoises. *Order Tubulidentata:* aardvark. *Order Proboscidea:* elephants and hyraxes. *Order Sirenia:* dugongs and manatees. *Order Perissodactyla:* horses, tapirs and rhinoceroses. *Order Artiodactyla:* pigs, camels, llamas, cattle, deer, giraffes, hippopotamuses and sheep.

Classification of the Plant Kingdom

Division Fungi: non-flowering plants lacking the green pigment chlorophyll, and which therefore do not make their own food; they obtain their food by absorbing the juices of dead matter (as saprophytes) or living matter (as parasites); plant body is a mass of threads called a mycelium. *Class Mycetozoa:* slime moulds; primitive jelly-like fungi. *Class Phycomycetes:* simple mycelium, free-living and parasitic forms. *Class Ascomycetes:* largest group of fungi; spores produced in a club-shaped ascus; includes the yeasts and truffles. *Class Basidiomycetes:* includes the familiar mushrooms and toadstools as well as the earthstars, puffballs and rusts.

Division Lichenes: lichens; plants formed by the close

association of a fungus (usually an Ascomycete) with an alga (usually a green, or blue-green variety); the fungus provides anchorage and absorbs minerals and water, the alga makes food and passes some to the fungus; lichens often appear as black, green or yellow growths on rocks and trees.

Division Algae: non-flowering plants ranging from single-celled forms to large, multicellular seaweeds; algae can be classified according to the colour of the pigments they contain. *Class Cyanophyta:* blue-green algae; single-celled or filamentous forms. *Class Chlorophyta:* green algae; ranging from single-celled to branched and lettuce-like forms; includes green seaweeds. *Class Xanthophyta:* forms possessing unequal whip-lash flagella. *Class Chrysophyta:* very large class, includes members of the plankton. *Class Bacillariophyta:* diatoms; part of the plankton. *Class Rhodophyta:* red algae; includes the red seaweeds – mainly deep water varieties. *Class Phaeophyta:* brown algae; commonest seaweeds on most rocky shores; includes the kelps and wracks.

Division Bryophyta: small, non-flowering plants often found in damp places. *Class Hepaticae:* liverworts; prostrate plants attached to the ground by root-like rhizoids. *Class Anthocerotae:* hornworts. *Class Musci:* mosses, usually erect plants with spiral leaves.

Division Pteridophyta: non-flowering plants with true stems, leaves and tissues, mainly terrestrial. *Class Psilopsida:* similar to earliest land plants; creeping stems and poorly developed leaves. *Class Lycopsida:* clubmosses. *Class Sphenopsida:* horsetails; ribbed, jointed stems bear whorls of leaves. *Class Pteropsida:* ferns; usually feathery plants; some aquatic forms.

Division Gymnospermae: primitive seed plants; unprotected ovules are borne in cones; commonly evergreen trees.

120

Class Cycadopsida: cycads; common trees in the tropics. *Class Coniferopsida:* conifers; trees with needle-like leaves; common trees in cool places. *Class Gnetopsida:* ovules are borne in flower-like structures, not cones; includes bizarre desert forms.

Division Angiospermae: higher, or flowering, plants; ovules are enclosed inside the protective ovary; most abundant plants on land, ranging from the familiar flowers, to bushes and trees. *Class Monocotyledoneae:* plants with one seed leaf (cotyledon) in the embryo; includes cereals, grasses, palms, lilies, daffodils, irises and orchids. *Class Dicotyledoneae:* plants with two seed leaves (cotyledons) in the embryo; includes deciduous trees (such as oak, beech, walnut and birch), fruit trees, food plants (such as potatoes, beans, cabbages and carrots), and an enormous variety of bushes, shrubs and flowers (such as roses, tulips, ivy, nettles, honeysuckles; daisies, heathers, rhododendrons and geraniums.

The Evolution of Life

The earth has been in existence for over 4,500 million years, and for much of that time no life existed. To begin with, harsh winds and violent rain storms lashed the earth, and a vast sea covered much of its surface.

The first scant signs of life have been discovered in rocks about 2,000 million years old, and were primitive kinds of bacteria. Although we do not know exactly how life began, we imagine that certain chemicals were present at the dawn of life, and that somehow the chemicals from this 'primaeval soup' combined together in such a way that living matter was formed.

Eventually, as conditions on earth slowly changed, new forms of life developed to exploit the new conditions. Some groups were able to live on almost unchanged because conditions changed only very little. This is true of the sharks, which have been the dominant life forms in the sea for hundreds of millions of years. On land, the story was different. The wet,

121

Era	Period	Millions of years ago	Animals	Plants
Cainozoic	Quaternary	2	man	
Cainozoic	Tertiary	70	apes monkeys bats whales dolphins marsupials rats camels insectivores sloths anteaters bears	
Mesozoic	Cretaceous	135	snakes birds early mammals	angiosperms yews cycads
Mesozoic	Jurassic	195	lizards crocodiles	early seed plants
Mesozoic	Triassic	225	dinosaurs newts gliding reptiles frogs toads salamanders turtles octopuses	ginkgoes
Palaeozoic	Permian	280	mammal-like reptiles belemnoids early reptiles	conifers
Palaeozoic	Carboniferous	345	early amphibians scorpions spiders ticks	early gymnosperms tree ferns
Palaeozoic	Devonian	395	bony fish lobe finned fish insects skates chitons rays sharks	fungi bryophytes seed ferns mosses ferns horsetails club mosses
Palaeozoic	Silurian	440	ammonoids oysters crabs armour plated fish prawns mussels lobsters	psilopsids early land plants
Palaeozoic	Ordovician	506	jawless fish whelks limpets topshells ostracods sea squirts	
Palaeozoic	Cambrian	606	tusk shells sea urchins starfish flatworms nautiloids sea cucumbers worms corals trilobites jellyfish bryozoans hydroids brachiopods protozoans sponges	seaweeds
Precambrian			flagellates bacteria	

warm climate of the Carboniferous and Permian became drier, and so the many types of amphibians which had flourished had to meet this change. Some types died out forever, but from other types, the reptiles were evolved. Later still, conditions suited the rise of the mammals – active, warm-blooded creatures with the ability to control their own body temperature.

Evolution is a continuing process, and although the present conditions on earth have allowed mammals (and especially man) to dominate the animal kingdom, and angiosperms to dominate the plant kingdom, perhaps in millions of years to come, their place will have been taken by new forms. The chart opposite shows, in geological time, the point at which the main groups of animals and plants had become established. A line over the name of a group means that it is extinct.

Nature Study

There is no substitute for studying nature in the wild, and most of us have the opportunity to see many different kinds of living things wherever we live. In cities there are usually parks where wildlife abounds, and those of us with gardens can do much to encourage birds and even small mammals like hedgehogs into them by putting out food – especially at times of the year when natural food is scarce. If you live in the country, the chances of discovering wildlife are even greater, but wherever you are, it all depends upon a sensible approach.

Firstly, go quietly or wait somewhere where you think an animal will visit. Most animals are shy and retiring, and loud voices or heavy footsteps will send them running or flying for shelter before you even get near. Learn the types of habitat and the times of the year when certain animals or plants are likely to be found. For instance it is no good looking for fungi in dry, open places in spring. You may find a few, but woodlands in late summer and autumn are much better places to look.

Often the only sign of wildlife is a discarded nest, or droppings, or the indication that an animal has been feeding – such as the remains of a pine cone that a squirrel leaves. Many interesting sights can be seen by peering through grass – this is just the place that small wild flowers may be growing – or by looking under piles of leaves, or under rotting bark. Try to join a local naturalists society. In addition to newsletters that tell you about interesting events in the region, you will find that it is possible to gain access to protected areas, and a warden will often take you on a useful 'tour'.

It is always a good idea to make notes about where you have been, what the weather was like and what you saw. In this way, you can compare these notes with new discoveries, and build up a picture of wildlife in your area.

Finally, this short section on nature study would be incomplete without a mention of two most valuable aids. Over the last few years some excellent field guides have been produced on almost all forms of wildlife. Properly used, these inexpensive items will increase your pleasure enormously by enabling you to identify most of the plants and animals you encounter. The second item is a pair of binoculars. For birdwatching they are almost essential if you are to see more than a few of the less shy varieties. Buy the best you can afford (or wait until your birthday or Christmas), and choose a pair with '8 × 30' stamped on them. These are light to handle and useful for watching birds and other forms of wildlife such as deer, rabbits and other mammals.

Nature Projects

There are many simple, practical projects that make nature study even more interesting. Here are a few which will also enable you to make attractive displays to keep.

Leaf rubbings Take a leaf from a common tree such as lime, beech or willow, and turn the upper (shiny) surface face down on a firm surface. Place a thin piece of paper over the leaf and go over it with a soft pencil or crayon. Soon the pattern of the leaf will emerge on the paper.

Bark rubbings To make a bark rubbing, hold a sheet of thick white paper against the bark of a tree (try and choose one which doesn't have too many deep cracks or fissures in it) and go over the paper with a soft pencil or crayon.

Spore prints Under the cap of a mushroom are millions of tiny spores, which are shed to produce new mushrooms. The spores are positioned between thin folds called gills. If you put a fresh mushroom cap gills downward onto a piece of white paper and leave it for 24 hours, many spores will have fallen from the cap onto the paper. The pattern will show the arrangement of the spores on the mushroom's gills.

Shell collections A visit to a sandy or rocky seashore is an exciting time, and there are always lots of different shells to collect. The shells were once the homes of molluscs, and the common types can be divided into two main types. Those which are usually spirally shaped and have a hole at the bottom (gastropod shells), and those that are usually flattish and round or oval shaped. These shells belonged to bivalve molluscs; the shell is in two parts, hinged together. Sometimes both parts can be found.

You can easily display a shell collection by cleaning the shells and gluing them to a piece of stiff card. Place all the gastropod shells together, then group all the bivalve shells together. Put the names of each underneath if you know them.

You may like to extend the display further to include seabird feathers, starfish skins, crab shells, cuttlebone (the internal shell of a mollusc called the cuttlefish) and pieces of seaweed.

Shells can also be glued to bottles and boxes to make interesting and attractive decorations.

Seaweed pictures Many of the beautiful seaweeds that are

125

found on the seashore can make very attractive 'pictures'. Wash the seaweed in a dish of water, and then gently place it on a piece of plain white paper. A paint brush is useful for 'teasing out' the fronds of the more delicate species. As the seaweed dries it will adhere to the paper. It can then be glued to a piece of cardboard for a permanent display.

Oak tree ecology display Many trees provide a home for a variety of other plants and animals, and none more so than the oak tree. An attractive display that will show a year in the life of an oak tree can be made as follows:

1. First, mark out on a piece of white card 4 equal quarters, and label them spring, summer, autumn and winter.
2. Make leaf prints (see previous page) during spring, summer and autumn. Draw each leaf also, using coloured crayons. Place each in the section according to the season.
3. Draw a twig with buds and place it in the winter section.
4. Make a bark rubbing (see previous page) and place it in the winter section.
5. Collect feathers from near the tree at each season. Try and identify them and glue them on the board.
6. Make notes about any birds or mammals (such as squirrels) that you have seen on the tree, and make short reports to place on the appropriate sections.
7. Look for any food remains that might give clues about other animals visiting the tree.
8. Collect an acorn and glue it on the autumn section.
9. During spring and summer look very carefully among the bark and leaves for the many small insects, caterpillars and spiders that live on the oak tree. Try and identify them and list the species that appear in each season. You may find it easier to hold a large piece of paper under a small branch, and then shake the insects onto it.
10. Look for any epiphytes (plants which grow on other plants) such as moss and lichens. Draw them and note where on the tree they were found.

126

OUTDOOR ACTIVITIES

Use of the Road

The open road is yours—on your bicycle or on foot—but your right to use it involves responsibilities on your part in return.

Cyclists, though they don't have to pass a driving test, must be fully aware of the Highway Code for their own safety as well as that of others. They are also obliged *by law* to have efficient brakes on *both* wheels, and a means of warning (either a bell or a horn). After dark they *must* have a head-lamp, a red tail-lamp and a red reflector at the rear. Cyclists are also advised to wear light-coloured clothes at night—and this is a safety measure for those on foot as well, particularly in country districts where because of the absence of a pavement it is necessary to walk along the edge of the road. Whenever walking on the road, whether by day or by night, you should *face* the oncoming traffic.

Cyclists should give clear hand-signals before making left or right turns, by raising the appropriate arm shoulder-high. On slowing down or stopping, the correct signal is an up-and-down movement of the right arm.

What the Highway Code tells you can be roughly summarised as follows:

For Pedestrians

1. Where there is no footpath, walk *facing* oncoming traffic.
2. Before crossing the road, look right, look left, then look right again. Cross at right-angles, use zebra crossings, central refuges or other pedestrian aids whenever possible, and take extra care if your view is limited or blocked in any way.

3. Before stepping onto a zebra crossing, allow approaching traffic ample time to stop. Remember that when a zebra crossing has a central refuge each half of the crossing must be treated separately.
4. At junctions, always watch for vehicles turning the corner.
5. If there is a police officer controlling traffic, be guided by his signals.
6. Do not get on or off any moving vehicle.

For Cyclists

1. When moving off, make the signal for a right turn before pulling out from the kerb.
2. Keep well to the left, except when overtaking or turning right.
3. Always, in riding at night, make sure you could pull up within the range of your lights. If dazzled by oncoming lights, slow down or stop.
4. Slow down before bends and sharp corners.
5. Give way to pedestrians on zebra crossings. They have the legal right of way. At crossings controlled by lights or police, give way to pedestrians already on the crossing when the signal to move is given.
6. When making a turn at a junction, remember that pedestrians who are crossing have the right of way.
7. Look out for pedestrians on country roads, and give them ample room, particularly at left-hand bends.
8. Go slow when passing animals, and give them plenty of room.
9. Do not overtake near corners, road junctions or pedestrian crossings, or when approaching the brow of a hill, a humpback bridge or a narrower section of road. Be extremely careful about overtaking at dusk or in fog.
10. Overtake on the right, except when the driver or rider in front has signalled that he intends to turn right.
11. Never cross a continuous white line along the middle of the road unless you can see a clear road ahead.

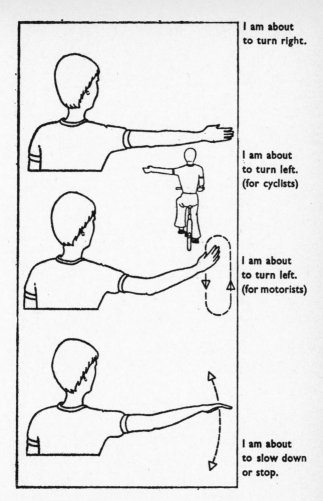

I am about
to turn right.

I am about
to turn left.
(for cyclists)

I am about
to turn left.
(for motorists)

I am about
to slow down
or stop.

129

12. When approaching a road junction where there is a 'Slow' sign, slow down and be prepared to stop if necessary. At a 'Halt' sign you *must* stop at the major road, even if it is clear.
13. To turn right, signal in good time and take up a position just left of the middle of the road. For left turns keep over to the left, signal well in advance and avoid swinging out to the right.
14. When you draw up, pull in close to the near side of the road.
15. When riding, glance behind before you signal, move off, change course, overtake or turn.
16. Slow down, look both ways and listen carefully before going through a railway level crossing that has no gates. When there are unattended gates, open both gates before crossing, then close them after you. *Do not stop on the lines.* Never cross the lines when a warning signal is flashing or when the barriers have not lifted after the passing of a train—another train may be on the way.
17. If there is a track for cycles, use it.
18. *Never* ride more than two abreast, carry anything which could interfere with your control of your bicycle, hold on to another vehicle or cyclist, or ride close behind a moving vehicle.
19. It is against the law to stop a bicycle within the limits of a pedestrian crossing, except in circumstances beyond your control or to avoid an accident.
20. It is illegal to ride on a footpath, or to carry a passenger on a bicycle not built or adapted for more than one.
21. It is illegal to ride recklessly, to interrupt the free passage of another road user or to leave your cycle on the road in such a way that it could cause danger to others.

Camping

Camping can prove to be an inexpensive and satisfying means of enjoying a superb holiday in beautiful parts of the country where it might otherwise be difficult to find suitable accommodation. It can also be hard work, uncomfortable and depressing, particularly if the weather is bad. Discomfort can be avoided, however, if you plan your holiday carefully and make sure that you have everything you need and nothing that you don't need. The equipment you take with you will depend upon whether you are backpacking (a walking trip carrying everything you need in a rucksack) or travelling by another means of transport to a place of your choice and establishing a longer-term camp. It will also depend upon the type of terrain in which you are camping – remember that mountains are dangerous in all weathers!

Whatever kind of camping you decide upon, you will find the following items of equipment useful:

tent, pegs and mallet
foam campamat
sleeping bag with sheet lining
pillow
gas lantern
gas cooking stove
fuel and matches
plastic or aluminium plates, mugs and bowls
saucepans, frying pan and kettle (all lightweight with folding
    handles for camping)
eggcups
cutlery
can and bottle opener
washing-up bowl and liquid
water carrier
scouring pads and drying-up cloths
airtight food box for perishable foods
lightweight folding stools for extra comfort

Camping Equipment

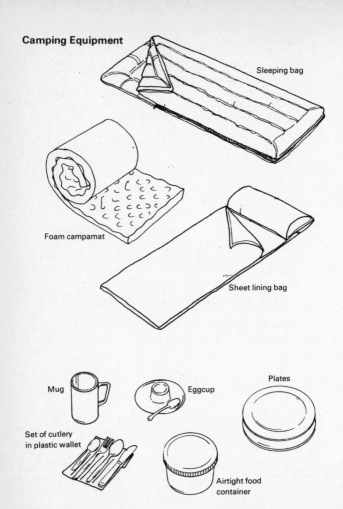

Sleeping bag

Foam campamat

Sheet lining bag

Mug

Eggcup

Plates

Set of cutlery
in plastic wallet

Airtight food
container

132

Lightweight folding stool

Plastic food boxes

Gas cartridge
cooking stove

Nest of billycans,
with frying pan lids

Kettle with
folding handle

Selection of
collapsible
water carriers

Gas lantern

133

polythene bags

first-aid kit

You will also need the following personal gear:

rucksack (of the highpack or anatomic type)

two complete sets of warm clothing including underwear and
socks (wool is best for everything)

the best boots you can afford

waterproofs (proofed nylon cagoule, for example)

maps and plastic map case to protect maps, especially in wet
weather

a good quality compass

torch (and spare batteries)

whistle

spare food and water

large polythene bag for emergency bivouac

personal wash bag and toiletries

towel

pocket knife

Before you do any camping, it is a good idea to talk to an
experienced person about equipment; also remember to follow
the country code.

Country Code

Whenever you are in the country you should follow the country
code which says that you should:

1. guard against all risks of fire;
2. leave no litter, take it home;
3. fasten all gates;
4. safeguard water supplies;
5. keep dogs under proper control;
6. protect wildlife, wild plants and trees;
7. keep to paths across farmland;
8. avoid damaging fences, hedges and walls;
9. go carefully on country roads;
10. respect the life of the countryside.

Tents

There are many types of tents to choose from but they are not cheap and you should decide carefully which type best suits your needs. A few are illustrated below.

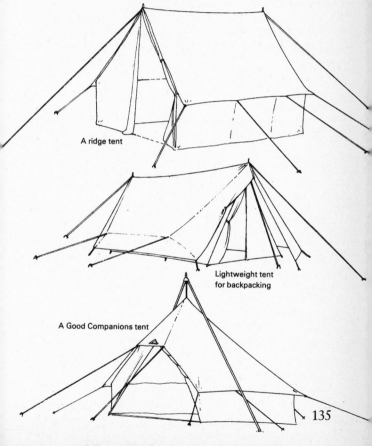

A ridge tent

Lightweight tent for backpacking

A Good Companions tent

135

Youth Hostels

Anyone wishing to use Youth Hostels can get full details of membership from their national headquarters.

The rules do vary slightly from country to country. In Britain anyone from the age of five years can join the Youth Hostels Association but up to the age of nine must be accompanied by their parent or guardian of the same sex or, in exceptional cases, by a responsible person over the age of eighteen of the same sex. Members between the ages of nine and twelve must be accompanied by a person over the age of eighteen who is also a member of the YHA.

There is a family membership scheme whereby children between five and sixteen are enrolled free if both parents (or widow or widower) join. If you live in England and Wales, your membership will be valid in more than forty countries and you will be one of more than 200,000 members. You may stay up to three consecutive nights at any one hostel and you may now arrive by car although the Association would prefer you to travel under your own steam. A list of national headquarters follows.

England and Wales Trevelyan House, 8 St Stephens Hill, St Albans, Herts AL1 2DY

Scotland 7 Glebe Crescent, Stirling FK8 2JA

Northern Ireland 93 Dublin Road, Belfast BT2 7HF

Eire 39 Mountjoy Square, Dublin 1

For members wishing to use hostels outside the British Isles consult YHA Services, 29 John Adam Street, London WC2N 6JE.

Australia 383 George Street, Sydney, New South Wales 2000

New Zealand PO Box 436, Christchurch C1

Canada 333 River Road, Vanier City, Ottawa, K1L 8B9 Ontario

USA National Campus, Delaplane, Virginia, 22025

Map reading

We have stressed in a previous section the importance of carrying, and knowing how to use, a map and compass. Being able to map read properly is helpful on a ramble, of course, but in barren, mountainous country or in areas where you must stay on footpaths, it is vital. Too many people embark on walks in the hills without wearing the proper clothes, without a map, let alone a compass, and with no idea of how the weather conditions can change. When they find themselves in danger, mountain rescue teams are obliged to put their own lives at risk to rescue them.

Most countries have been surveyed so that maps are available for many areas of the world, but perhaps Britain is as well covered as any. In Britain maps are available from the Ordnance Survey and can be bought in many good book shops or branches of Her Majesty's Stationery Office. The most useful have a scale of either 1:50 000 or 1:25 000. Firstly, you must know what all the signs and symbols on the map mean; this part is easy, all the symbols are explained carefully on the edge of the map itself. The symbols shown on a 1:50 000 scale ordnance map are shown on the following two pages. If you have a good sense of direction and you are walking in an area where there are plenty of easily recognisable features, a map may be enough, but most of the time, it is more sensible to carry a compass.

There are many different kinds of compass on the market and you can even make a very crude one for yourself by magnetising a needle, pushing it through a piece of cork, and floating it on a saucer of water – the needle will always align itself north/south – but this is neither accurate enough nor very convenient. The best type to buy is the Silva protractor type which, despite the name, is really very easy to use, and is robust and reliable; it comes with a full set of instructions for its use. But be warned, it is not cheap! There is not sufficient space here to describe the easiest and most efficient ways to use a map and compass but there are books available on the subject. A book that explains

137

Ordnance Survey Map Symbols Scale 1 : 50000

Roads and paths

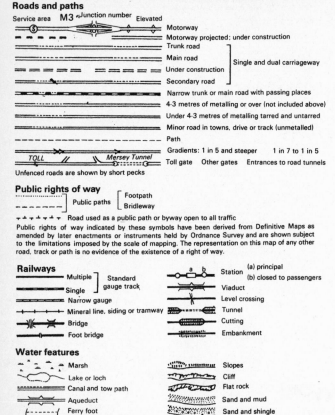

Service area   M3   Junction number   Elevated

Motorway

Motorway projected; under construction

Trunk road

Main road

Under construction   } Single and dual carriageway

Secondary road

Narrow trunk or main road with passing places

4·3 metres of metalling or over (not included above)

Under 4·3 metres of metalling tarred and untarred

Minor road in towns, drive or track (unmetalled)

Path

Gradients: 1 in 5 and steeper   1 in 7 to 1 in 5

TOLL   Mersey Tunnel

Toll gate   Other gates   Entrances to road tunnels

Unfenced roads are shown by short pecks

Public rights of way

Public paths   [Footpath
                  [Bridleway

Road used as a public path or byway open to all traffic

Public rights of way indicated by these symbols have been derived from Definitive Maps as amended by later enactments or instruments held by Ordnance Survey and are shown subject to the limitations imposed by the scale of mapping. The representation on this map of any other road, track or path is no evidence of the existence of a right of way.

Railways

Multiple   } Standard
Single   gauge track
Narrow gauge
Mineral line, siding or tramway
Bridge
Foot bridge

Station   (a) principal
            (b) closed to passengers
Viaduct
Level crossing
Tunnel
Cutting
Embankment

Water features

Marsh
Lake or loch
Canal and tow path
Aqueduct
Ferry foot
Ferry vehicle
Foot bridge
Light vessel, lighthouse and beacon

Slopes
Cliff
Flat rock
Sand and mud
Sand and shingle
Low water mark
High water mark
Highest point to which tides flow

138

General features

〜⤬〜⤬〜 Electricity transmission line
(with pylons spaced conventionally)

>‒ ‒> ‒ >‒ ‒> Pipe line
(arrow indicates direction of flow)

⊲⊗⊳ Quarry

◌◌ Open pit

⌒⌒⌒ Wood

▨▨▨ Orchard

▤▤▤ Park or ornamental grounds

 Bracken, heath and rough grassland

⋰⋰⋰ Dunes

λ Broadcasting station (mast or tower)

⊃⊂ Bus or coach station

⛪ Church ⎡ with tower

⛪ or ⎢ with spire

+ Chapel ⎣ without tower or spire

⌂ Glasshouse

+ Graticule intersection at 5′ intervals

△ Triangulation pillar

☼ Windmill (in use)

☋ Windmill (disused)

⊥ Wind pump

▲ Youth hostel

Relief

―― 80 ―― Contour values are given to the nearest
metre. The vertical interval is, however,
50 feet.

·144 Heights are to the nearest metre above
mean sea level. Heights shown close to a
triangulation pillar refer to the station
height at ground level and not necessarily
to the summit. Details of the summit
height may be obtained from
the Ordnance Survey.

1 metre = 3·2808 feet

15·24 metres = 50 feet

Boundaries

—+—+—+ National

-O-O-O-O- London Borough

———— National Park
County or

—·—·—·— Metropolitan County

·················· Civil Parish or
equivalent

Abbreviations

P Post office

PH Public house

CH Club house

·MP Mile post

·MS Mile stone

TH Town hall, Guildhall or equivalent

PC Public convenience (in rural areas)

·T ⎡ PO

·A Telephone call box ⎢ AA

·R ⎣ RAC

Antiquities

VILLA Roman

Cumulus Non-Roman

+ Site of antiquity

⚔ Battlefield (with date)
1066

all you need to know clearly and simply is the *Reading Maps* (Metric edition), title in the Macdonald's Geography series. For very much more detailed information refer to *Ordnance Survey Maps, A Descriptive Manual* by J.B. Harley which you should find in the reference section of any good library.

One very important point to remember when you are using a map and compass is to allow for the magnetic deviation. This is the difference in degrees between the position of the magnetic north pole and the geographic north pole. Obviously this will vary depending upon the latitude in which you are walking. Here, again, the map will tell you the difference between true and magnetic north, so do not forget to look and bear it in mind.

The Silva Compass

To take a bearing with a Silva compass, stand squarely facing the object, holding the compass in front of you in one hand and point the direction line at the object. Turn the scale with your other hand so that the compass needle points to the zero mark. The magnetic bearing can be read where the scale of degrees meets the direction line.

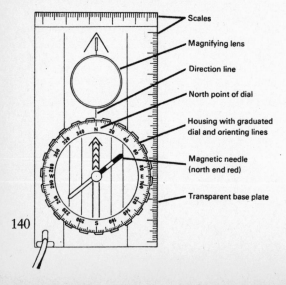

Scales

Magnifying lens

Direction line

North point of dial

Housing with graduated dial and orienting lines

Magnetic needle (north end red)

Transparent base plate

140

Anatomic backpack

Waterproof nylon cagoule

Woollen knee socks

Strong walking boots

Rambling

It seems to be the case that the more people are confined to town dwelling and the further they are removed from any direct association with the countryside, such as farming or the like, then the more popular rambling becomes. *The Hamlyn Encyclopedic World Dictionary* defines rambling as wandering about in a leisurely manner without definite aim or direction, or walking for pleasure. And there is no doubt that a stroll in beautiful countryside, perhaps with no destination in mind other than returning home tired but satisfied at the end of the day, can be very enjoyable, indeed. Then there is the pleasure of observing the natural world around you: to see hares sparring with one another in a ploughed field in spring; to find a rare orchid half hidden in the undergrowth; to hear a nightingale's song along a woodland edge in the evening.

The countryside is not a playground, however. It is living, growing and changing, just like you or I. And just like you or I, it can be harmed by the careless action or the wilful deed – a bottle tossed away after an enjoyable picnic can trap and kill many a curious vole or shrew; leaving open a field gate can allow cattle into a field of lush vegetation which they might devour hungrily and then become bloated or even die; picking a bunch of wild flowers might mean that there will be none next year. So be careful and thoughtful, stay on footpaths, and follow the country code. Try to understand and respect the countryside – you will find that it is worth the trouble.

Whenever you go walking, particularly in remote or mountainous country, you should always wear the correct clothes and carry a map and compass – and know how to use them! In rough country, make sure that you are wearing strong but comfortable boots, and try to break them in before you undertake a long walk. Wear clothes that are warm and loose fitting, preferably made of wool, and take a spare sweater and socks – in the mountains the conditions can change very rapidly. Don't forget waterproofs and spare food and water, too. And check the weather forecast before you set off. It is always important to leave your name and estimated time of return with someone so that if you do not return someone will know – and do tell them your intended route so that they will know where to look if you do get into difficulty. But you might just be taking an evening stroll across your local fields, in which case you need worry less about personal safety, but still respect and enjoy the country.

You may prefer to walk in organised parties with people who have similar interests to your own. In Britain you can join the Ramblers' Association by writing to 1–4 Crawford Mews, York Street, London W1H 1PT, and they will put you in touch with your local group.

Orienteering

Orienteering as a sport first took place in Scandinavia and was introduced into Britain in 1962. It is an activity in which all the family can take part – including parents pushing their child in a pushchair! The idea is to test the speed and accuracy with which you can find your way around a course of perhaps eight or ten kilometres (five or six miles) in unfamiliar terrain following a route of control points which have only been given to you a few minutes before the event starts. You will have a map and compass and it is the skill with which you are able to use these which may decide whether you win or lose a competition. It is not always the fittest person, able to run the distance easily,

142

that wins, and a slower more methodical approach may pay dividends. Obviously, however, it helps if you are in good physical shape, too.

People are attracted to orienteering for a variety of reasons: many who live in industrialised areas are only too glad to take the opportunity of getting away from it all into the more peaceful surroundings of the wilderness; many are glad of the chance to observe nature in action; then there are those who relish the idea of pitting their navigating skills and fitness against other competitors. Whatever your reasons turn out to be, whenever you are in the country do not forget to observe the country code and remember to encourage the other competitors to do the same. Large numbers of people can do a great deal of damage to wild life and farming interests if they do not take care.

There are different types of events in which an orienteer can take part. For example, Ordinary Events are designed for anyone between the ages of ten years to sixty years, whereas the Wayfarers' Course caters for complete beginners or the very young and takes place along main tracks avoiding difficult or dangerous terrain. If you wish to take part in orienteering the first thing to do is to get in touch with your nearest group and your local library or school should be able to help you there. In Britain, you can write to the British Orienteering Federation, Lea Green, Matlock, Derbyshire DE4 5GJ. There is also an International Orienteering Federation.

These organisations will be able to tell you the equipment you will need but, in general, you will require a whistle, a reliable ball-point pen or waterproof pencil, and a compass, preferably of the protractor type already mentioned. You will also require suitable clothing, including waterproofs and, perhaps most important, the right kind of footwear. This must depend upon what is comfortable for you but many orienteers recommend studded, not spiked, running shoes.

At whatever level you wish to enter into this sport perhaps the most important thing is that you should enjoy yourself.

143

THE WORLD OF SPORT

People and Sport

Sport is an important part of life in the twentieth century. As a topic of conversation among friends and acquaintances it is second to none, and it takes increasing space in newspapers and magazines.

What is its purpose? It has many. It provides pleasure for the participants and entertainment for spectators. It allows sportsmen and sportswomen to express themselves. As well as providing them with the exhilaration of developing and achieving skills admired by all, it keeps them fit. A fit body leads to a keen mind, as the Latin proverb says: *mens sana in corpore sano*.

One need not be good at sports to enjoy them. According to the Olympic ideal it is the taking part, not the winning, which is important. Not being a perfect world, this ideal is often forgotten, particularly when national pride is at stake. Communist countries are frequently accused of over intensive coaching of young sportsmen and sportswomen with a view to winning medals for the prestige of their countries. Nadia Comaneci and Kornelia Ender are young girls who, according to Western critics, might have sacrificed some of the pleasures of a normal childhood in order to be coached for Olympic greatness.

In the West, it might be charged that professionalism has had the same effect on the top sportsmen and women. So much money can now be earned by the best, that winning has become far more important than taking part.

So far as young people are concerned, sport should be fun. There is great satisfaction in doing one's best. In team games, friendship and team-spirit are pleasures which last after the game has finished. In lonely pursuits like athletics, there is much to be learned by the young person who runs or jumps to his or her physical limits. It is not fanciful to say that taking part in sports makes a boy or girl not only healthier and fitter but better disciplined and more aware of the strengths and limitations of his or her body.

Girls nowadays have more opportunities for enjoying sports than their grandmothers ever did. Only in the last fifty years or so have shorts or short dresses been seen in the women's tennis championships at Wimbledon. Even well-remembered champions like Suzanne Lenglen played in ankle-length skirts.

In most sports, the best men, because of their physique, are better than the best women. There is reason to believe that this will always be the case. In some sports, this difference matters less than in others. In 1977 Charlotte Brew became the first woman to ride in the Grand National Steeplechase. She did not do well, and some experts suggest that a woman will never have the strength to win this race. Time will tell. Certainly in show-jumping and three-day eventing women now compete on equal terms with the men.

Nowadays sporting records get broken with much more regularity than they did in the past, and it is exceptional for an Olympic record, for instance, to survive the following Olympics. In this section are listed some of the records of the world's most popular sporting events.

Athletics

More than seven hundred years before the birth of Christ, the Olympic Games were a regular feature of Greek life. Although they were abolished in the fourth century AD, men and women never lost their pleasure in matching their speeds against each other in races, or their strength in jumping or throwing. By the nineteenth century there was a revival in competitive sports with schools and universities staging championships, and the innovation of the modern Olympic Games in 1896 made athletics once again a sport for millions to enjoy all over the world.

Nowadays, some argue that the Olympic Games, which are

held every four years and rival the World Cup Finals as the world's biggest and most avidly followed sporting spectacle, are too big. The 1972 Munich games, for example, were used for political purposes, with the massacre of Israeli athletes and Black Power demonstrations. The 1976 games suffered because some black African athletes, among them some of the best in the world, like Filbert Bayi, were not allowed to take part because New Zealand, who had had sporting contact with South Africa, were participating. The games, in a sporting sense, are also slightly unfair in that a top athlete might reach his or her peak in the four-year period between games or be injured at the crucial time, and be deprived of a gold medal merely by an accident of timing. However, while they exist in their present form, they are the best indication of who is the best in the world at all the events.

World records (men)

In 1976 the International Amateur Athletics Federation congress committee decided to recognise world records for events up to and including distances of 400 metres only if the record claimed had been timed electrically. The following list therefore includes only official (i.e. electrically timed) world records for those events. Were hand timing recognised, some of the records could be lower.

Event	Holder	Nation	Record	Year
100 m	Jim Hines	USA	9.95 s	1968
200 m	Tommie Smith	USA	19.83 s	1968
400 m	Lee Evans	USA	43.86 s	1968
800 m	Alberto Juantorena	Cuba	1 min 43.44 s	1976
1500 m	Filbert Bayi	Tanzania	3 min 32.20 s	1974
5000 m	Henry Rono	Kenya	13 min 08.4 s	1978

Event	Holder	Nation	Record	Year
10000 m	Henry Rono	Kenya	27 min 22.5 s	1978
110 m hurdles	Alessandro Casanas	Cuba	13.21 s	1977
400 m hurdles	Edwin Moses	USA	47.45 s	1977
3000 m steeplechase	Henry Rono	Kenya	8 min 05.4 s	1978
Marathon	Derek Clayton	Australia	2 hrs 8 min 34 s	1969
20 km walk	Daniel Bautista	Mexico	1 hr 23 min 39 s	1976
High jump	Vladimir Yaschenko	USSR	2.34 m	1977
Pole vault	Mike Tully	USA	5.71 m	1978
Long jump	Bob Beamon	USA	8.90 m	1968
Triple jump	J.C. de Oliveira	Brazil	17.89 m	1975
Shot	Udo Beyer	E. Germany	22.15 m	1978
Discus	Wolfgang Schmidt	E. Germany	71.16 m	1978
Hammer	Karl-Hans Riehm	W. Germany	80.32 m	1978
Javelin	Miklos Nemeth	Hungary	94.58 m	1976
Decathlon	Bruce Jenner	USA	8618 points	1976
4 × 100 m relay		USA	38.03 s	1977
4 × 400 m relay		USA	2 min 56.2 s	1968

World records (women)

Event	Holder	Nation	Record	Year
100 m	Marlies Goehr	E. Germany	10.88 s	1977
200 m	Marita Koch	E. Germany	22.06 s	1978
400 m	Marita Koch	E. Germany	49.02 s	1978

800 m	Tatiana Kazankina	USSR	1 min 54.94 s	1976
1500 m	Tatiana Kazankina	USSR	3 min 56 s	1976
100 m hurdles	Grazya Rabsztyn	Poland	12.48 s	1978
High jump	Sara Simeoni	Italy	2.01 m	1978
Long jump	Vilma Bardauskiene	USSR	7.09 m	1978
Shot	Helena Fibingerova	Czecho-slovakia	22.32 m	1977
Discus	Evelin Jahl	E. Germany	70.72 m	1978
Javelin	Kate Schmidt	USA	69.32 m	1977
Pentathlon	Burglinde Pollak	E. Germany	4932 points	1973
4 × 100 m relay		E. Germany	42.27 s	1978
4 × 400 m relay		E. Germany	3 min 19.23 s	1976

Olympic Champions

The reigning Olympic champions (1976 Games, Montreal) are as follows:

Men

100 m: Hasely Crawford (Trinidad and Tobago)
200 m: Don Quarrie (Jamaica)
400 m: Alberto Juantorena (Cuba)
800 m: Alberto Juantorena (Cuba)
1500 m: John Walker (New Zealand)
5000 m: Lasse Viren (Finland)
10000 m: Lasse Viren (Finland)
110 m hurdles: Guy Drut (France)
400 m hurdles: Edwin Moses (USA)
3000 m steeplechase: Anders Garderud (Sweden)
Marathon: Waldemar Cierpinski (E. Germany)

20 km walk: Daniel Bautista (Mexico)
High jump: Jacek Wszola (Poland)
Pole vault: Tadeusz Slusarski (Poland)
Long jump: Arnie Robinson (USA)
Triple jump: Valeri Saneyev (USSR)
Shot: Udo Beyer (E. Germany)
Discus: Mac Wilkins (USA)
Hammer: Yuriy Sedyh (USSR)
Javelin: Miklos Nemeth (Hungary)
Decathlon: Bruce Jenner (USA)

Women
100 m: Annegret Richter (W. Germany)
200 m: Baerbel Eckert (E. Germany)
400 m: Irena Szewinska (Poland)
800 m: Tatiana Kazankina (USSR)
1500 m: Tatiana Kazankina (USSR)
100 m hurdles: Johanna Schaller (E. Germany)
High jump: Rosemarie Ackermann (E. Germany)
Long jump: Anglea Voigt (E. Germany)
Shot: Ivanka Christova (Bulgaria)
Discus: Evelin Schlaak (E. Germany)
Javelin: Ruth Fuchs (E. Germany)
Pentathlon: Sigrun Siegl (E. Germany)

Gymnastics

The world, Olympic and European champions are as follows:
Men

Event	World champion (1978)	European champion (1975)	Olympic champion (1976)
Parallel bars	E. Kenmotsu (Japan)	N. Andrianov (USSR)	S. Kato (Japan)
Rings	N. Andrianov (USSR)	D. Grecu (Rumania)	N. Andrianov (USSR)

149

Event	World champion	European champion	Olympic champion
Vault	J. Shimizu (Japan)	N. Andrianov (USSR)	N. Andrianov (USSR)
Horizontal bar	S. Kasamatsu (Japan)	N. Andrianov (USSR) E. Gienger (W. Germany)	M. Tsukahara (Japan)
Floor	K. Thomas (USA)	N. Andrianov (USSR) A. Szajna (Poland)	N. Andrianov (USSR)
Pommel horse	Z. Magyar (Hungary)	Z. Magyar (Hungary)	Z. Magyar (Hungary)
Overall champion 1	N. Andrianov (USSR)	N. Andrianov (USSR)	N. Andrianov (USSR)
2	E. Kenmotsu (Japan)	E. Gienger (W. Germany)	S. Kato (Japan)
3	A. Detiatin (USSR)	A. Detiatin (USSR)	M. Tsukahara (Japan)

Women

Event	World champion (1978)	European champion (1975)	Olympic champion (1976
Vault	N. Kim (USSR)	N. Comaneci (Rumania)	N. Kim (USSR)
Beam	N. Comaneci (Rumania)	N. Comaneci (Rumania)	N. Comaneci (Rumania)
Assymetrical bars	M. Frederick (USA)	N. Comaneci (Rumania)	N. Comaneci (Rumania)
Floor	E. Moukhina (USSR) & N. Kim	N. Kim (USSR)	N. Kim (USSR)
Overall champion 1	E. Moukhina (USSR)	N. Comaneci (Rumania)	N. Comaneci (Rumania)
2	N. Kim (USSR)	N. Kim (USSR)	N. Kim (USSR)
3	N. Shaposhnikova (USSR)	A. Zinke (E. Germany)	L. Tourischeva (USSR)

Lawn Tennis

Lawn tennis arose out of the game of court tennis or real tennis, which has been played since the thirteenth century. It was invented by Major Walter Clopton Wingfield in 1874. In 1877 the first championships were held at Wimbledon. The Wimbledon championships were originally open only to amateurs, but after professionalism claimed many of the world's great players from the 1950s, Wimbledon was forced to become open to all in 1968. The Wimbledon championships are the premier championships of the world. The finals since 1950 are as follows:

Men's Singles

1960: Neale Fraser (Australia) beat Rod Laver (Australia) 6–4, 3–6, 9–7, 7–5

1961: Rod Laver (Australia) beat Chuck McKinley (USA) 6–3, 6–1, 6–4

1962: Rod Laver (Australia) beat Martin Mulligan (Australia) 6–2, 6–2, 6–1

1963: Chuck McKinley (USA) beat Fred Stolle (Australia) 9–7, 6–1, 6–4

1964: Roy Emerson (Australia) beat Fred Stolle (Australia) 6–4, 12–10, 4–6, 6–3

1965: Roy Emerson (Australia) beat Fred Stolle (Australia) 6–2, 6–4, 6–4

1966: Manuel Santana (Spain) beat Dick Ralston (USA) 6–4, 11–9, 6–4

1967: John Newcombe (Australia) beat Will Bungert (Germany) 6–3, 6–1, 6–1

1968: Rod Laver (Australia) beat Tony Roche (Australia) 6–3, 6–4, 6–2

1969: Rod Laver (Australia) beat John Newcombe (Australia) 6–4, 5–7, 6–4, 6–4

1970: John Newcombe (Australia) beat Ken Rosewall (Australia) 5–7, 6–3, 6–2, 3–6, 6–1

1971: John Newcombe (Australia) beat Stan Smith (USA) 6–3, 5–7, 2–6, 6–4, 6–4

1972: Stan Smith (USA) beat Ilie Nastase (Rumania) 4–6, 6–3, 6–3, 4–6, 7–5

1973: Jan Kodes (Czechoslovakia) beat Alex Metreveli (USSR) 6–1, 9–8, 6–3

1974: Jimmy Connors (USA) beat Ken Rosewall (Australia) 6–1, 6–1, 6–4

1975: Arthur Ashe (USA) beat Jimmy Connors (USA) 6–1, 6–1, 5–7, 6–4

1976: Bjorn Borg (Sweden) beat Ilie Nastase (Rumania) 6–4, 6–2, 9–7

1977: Bjorn Borg (Sweden) beat Jimmy Connors (USA) 3–6, 6–2, 6–1, 5–7, 6–4

1978: Bjorn Borg (Sweden) beat Jimmy Connors (USA) 6–2, 6–2, 6–3

Women's Singles

1960: Maria Bueno (Brazil) beat Sandra Reynolds (South Africa) 8–6, 6–0

1961: Angela Mortimer (Gt. Britain) beat Christine Truman (Gt. Britain) 4–6, 6–4, 7–5

1962: Mrs. J. R. Susman (USA) beat Mrs. V. Sukova (Czechoslovakia) 6–4, 6–4

1963: Margaret Smith (Australia) beat Billie Jean Moffitt (USA) 6–3, 6–4

1964: Maria Bueno (Brazil) beat Margaret Smith (Australia) 6–4, 7–9, 6–3

1965: Margaret Smith (Australia) beat Maria Bueno (Brazil) 6–4, 7–5

1966: Mrs. Billie Jean King (formerly Miss Moffitt) (USA) beat Maria Bueno (Brazil) 6–3, 3–6, 6–1

1967: Mrs. Billie Jean King (USA) beat Mrs. Ann Jones (Gt. Britain) 6–3, 6–4

1968: Mrs. Billie Jean King (USA) beat Judy Tegart (Australia) 9–7. 7–5
1969: Mrs. Ann Jones (Gt. Britain) beat Mrs. Billie Jean King (USA) 3–6, 6–3, 6–2
1970: Mrs. Margaret Court (formerly Miss Smith) (Australia) beat Mrs. Billie Jean King 14–12, 11–9
1971: Evonne Goolagong (Australia) beat Mrs. Margaret Court (Australia) 6–4, 6–1
1972: Mrs. Billie Jean King (USA) beat Evonne Goolagong (Australia) 6–3, 6–3
1973: Mrs. Billie Jean King (USA) beat Chris Evert (USA) 6–0, 7–5
1974: Christ Evert (USA) beat Mrs. Olga Morozova (USSR) 6–0, 6–4
1975: Mrs. Billie Jean King (USA) beat Mrs. Evonne Cawley (formerly Miss Goolagong) (Australia) 6–0, 6–1
1976: Chris Evert (USA) beat Mrs. Evonne Cawley (Australia) 6–3, 4–6, 8–6
1977: Virginia Wade (Gt. Britain) beat Betty Stove (Holland) 4–6, 6–3, 6–1
1978: Martina Navratilova (USA) beat Chris Evert (USA) 2–6, 6–4, 7–5

Men's Doubles (since 1970)

1970: Newcombe and Roche beat Rosewall and Stolle 10–8, 6–3, 6–1
1971: Emerson and Laver beat Ashe and Ralston 4–6, 9–7, 6–8, 6–4, 6–4
1972: Hewitt and McMillan beat Smith and Van Dillen 6–2, 6–2, 9–7
1973: Connors and Nastase beat Cooper and Fraser 3–6, 6–3, 6–4, 8–9, 6–1
1974: Newcombe and Roche beat Lutz and Smith 8–6, 6–4, 6–4
1975: Gerulaitis and Mayer beat Dowdeswell and Stone 7–5, 8–6, 6–4
1976: Gottfried and Ramirez beat Case and Masters 3–6, 6–3, 8–6, 2–6, 7–5

1977: Case and Masters beat Alexander and Dent 6–3, 6–4, 3–6, 8–9, 6–4

1978: Hewitt and McMillan beat Fleming and McEnroe 6–1, 6–4, 6–2

Women's Doubles (since 1970)

1970: Casals and King beat Durr and Wade 6–2, 6–3

1971: Casals and King beat Court and Goolagong 6–3, 6–2

1972: King and Stove beat Dalton and Durr 6–2, 4–6, 6–3

1973: Casals and King beat Durr and Stove 6–1, 4–6, 7–5

1974: Goolagong and Michel beat Gourlay and Krantzcke 2–6, 6–4, 6–3

1975: Kiyomura and Sawamatsu beat Durr and Stove 7–5, 1–6, 7–5

1976: Evert and Navratilova beat King and Stove 6–1, 3–6, 7–5

1977: Cawley (formerly Gourlay) and Russell beat Navratilova and Stove 6–3, 6–3

1978: Reid and Turnbull beat Javsovec and Ruzici 4–6, 9–8, 6–3

Mixed Doubles (since 1970)

1970: Nastase and Casals beat Metrevelli and Morozova 6–3, 4–6, 9–7

1971: Davidson and King beat Riessen and Court 3–6, 6–2, 15–13

1972: Nastase and Casals beat Warwick and Goolagong 6–4, 6–4

1973: Davidson and King beat Ramirez and Newbery 6–3, 6–2

1974: Davidson and King beat Farrell and Charles 6–3, 9–7

1975: Riessen and Court beat Stone and Stove 6–4, 7–5

1976: Roche and Durr beat Stockton and Casals 6–3, 2–6, 7–5

1977: Hewitt and Stevens beat McMillan and Stove 3–6, 7–5, 6–4

1978: McMillan and Stove beat Ruffels and King 6–2, 6–2

Davis Cup

The Davis Cup is the lawn tennis championship for nations. The results of the final round since 1970 are as follows:

1970: USA 5, Germany 0
1971: USA 3, Rumania 2
1972: USA 3, Rumania 2
1973: Australia 5, USA 0
1974: South Africa won (India scratched)
1975: Sweden 3, Czechoslovakia 2
1976: Italy 4, Chile 1
1977: Australia 3, Italy 1

Wightman Cup

The Wightman Cup is the women's lawn tennis team championship between Great Britain and the United States. The results since 1970 have been:

1970: USA 4, Gt. Britain 3
1971: USA 4, Gt. Britain 3
1972: USA 5, Gt. Britain 2
1973: USA 5, Gt. Britain 2
1974: Gt. Britain 6, USA 1
1975: Gt. Britain 5, USA 2
1976: USA 5, Gt. Britain 2
1977: USA 7, Gt. Britain 0
1978: Gt. Britain 4, USA 3

Federation Cup

The Federation Cup was inaugurated in London in 1963 to be the women's international team championship. The results of the final since its inception are as follows:

1963: USA 2, Australia 1
1964: Australia 2, USA 1
1965: Australia 2, USA 1
1966: USA 3, W. Germany 0

1967: USA 2, England 0
1968: Australia 3, Holland 0
1969: USA 2, Australia 1
1970: Australia 3, W. Germany 0
1971: Australia 3, England 0
1972: South Africa 2, England 1
1973: Australia 3, South Africa 0
1974: Australia 2, USA 1
1975: Czechoslovakia 3, Australia 0
1976: USA 2, Australia 1
1977: USA 2, Australia 1

Showjumping

Showjumping has been part of the Olympic Games since the
turn of the century and has achieved enormous popularity
since the war, particularly in Britain, where extensive television
coverage has helped to make the leading riders household
names. The records of the principal competitions follow.

Men's World Championships

1953: 1. F. Goyoaga (Spain) *Quorum*. 2. F. Thiedemann (Germany) *Diamant*. 3. P.J. d'Oriola (France) *Ali Baba*.
4. P. d'Inzeo (Italy) *Uruguay*.

1954: 1. H.G. Winkler (Germany) *Halla*. 2. P.J. d'Oriola
(France) *Arlequin*. 3. F. Goyoaga (Spain) *Quorum*.
4. S. Oppes (Italy) *Pagoro*.

1955: 1. H.G. Winkler (Germany) *Halla*. 2. R. d'Inzeo (Italy)
Nadir. 3. R. Dallas (Gt. Britain) *Bones*. 4. P.J. d'Oriola
(France) retired.

1956: 1. R. d'Inzeo (Italy) *Merano*. 2. F. Goyoaga (Spain)
Fahnenkonig. 3. F. Thiedemann (Germany) *Meteor*. 4.
C. Delia (Argentina) *Huipil*.

1960: 1. R. d'Inzeo (Italy) *Gowran Girl*. 2. C. Delia (Argentina) *Huipil*. 3. D. Broome (Gt. Britain) *Sunsalve*. 4 W. Steinkraus (USA) *Ksar d'Esprit*.
1966: 1. P.J. d'Oriola (France) *Pomone*. 2. A. de Bohorques (Spain) *Quizas*. 3. R. d'Inzeo (Italy) *Bowjak*. 4. N. Pessoa (Brazil) *Huipil*.
1970: 1. D. Broome (Gt. Britain) *Beethoven*. 2 G. Mancinelli (Italy) *Fidux*. 3. H. Smith (Gt. Britain) *Mattie Brown*. 4. A. Schockemohle (Germany) *Donald Rex*.
1974: 1. H. Steenken (Germany) *Simona*. 2. E. Macken (Ireland) *Pele*. 3. H. Simon (Austria) *Lavendel*. 4. F. Chapot (USA) *Main Spring*.
1978: 1. G. Wiltfang (Germany) *Roman*. 2. E. Macken (Ireland) *Boomerang*. 3. M. Matz (USA) *Jet Run*. 4. J. Heins (Netherlands) *Pandur*.

Women's World Championships
1965: 1. M. Coakes (Gt. Britain) *Stroller*. 2. K. Kusner (USA) *Untouchable*. 3. A. Westwood (Gt. Britain) *The Maverick*.
1970: 1. J. Lefebvre (France) *Rocket*. 2. Mrs. D. Mould (formerly Miss Coakes) (Gt. Britain) *Stroller*. 3. A. Drummond-Hay (Gt. Britain) *Merely-a-Monarch*.
1974: 1. Mme. J. Tissot (formerly Mlle Lefebvre) (France) *Rocket*. 2. M. McEvoy (USA) *Mr. Muskie*. 3. Mrs. B. Kerr (Canada) *Magnor*.

Men's European Championships (winners only)
1957: H.G. Winkler (Germany) *Sonnenglanz*
1958: F. Thiedemann (Germany) *Meteor*.
1959: P. d'Inzeo (Italy) *Uruguay*
1961: D. Broome (Gt. Britain) *Sunsalve*
1962: C.D. Barker (Gt. Britain) *Mister Softee*
1963: G. Mancinelli (Italy) *Rockette*
1965: H. Schridde (Germany) *Dozent*

1966: N. Pessoa (Brazil) *Gran Geste*
1967: D. Broome (Gt. Britain) *Mister Softee*
1969: D. Broome (Gt. Britain) *Mister Softee*
1971: H. Steenken (Germany) *Simona*
1973: P. McMahon (Gt. Britain) *Pennwood Forge Mill*

Championship for men and women (amateurs only)
1975: A. Schockemohle (Germany) *Warwick*
1977: J. Heins (Netherlands) *Pandur*

Women's European Championships (winners only)
1957: P. Smythe (Gt. Britain) *Flanagan*
1958: G. Serventi (Italy) *Doly*
1959: A. Townsend (Gt. Britain) *Bandit*
1960: S. Cohen (Gt. Britain) *Clare Castle*
1961: P. Smythe (Gt. Britain) *Flanagan*
1962: P. Smythe (Gt. Britain) *Flanagan*
1963: P. Smythe (Gt. Britain) *Flanagan*
1966: J. Lefebvre (France) *Kenavo*
1967: K. Kusner (USA) *Untouchable*
1968: A. Drummond-Hay (Gt. Britain) *Merely-a-Monarch*
1969: I. Kellett (Ireland) *Morning Light*
1971: A. Moore (Gt. Britain) *Psalm*
1973: A. Moore (Gt. Britain) *Psalm*
1975: See under Men's European championships

President's Cup
The President's Cup is the world team championship, and the

winners are decided by each country's six best Nation Cup results. Winners:

1965: Gt. Britain 35 points; Germany 31; Italy 30
1966: USA 27 points; Spain 26; France 20
1967: Gt. Britain 37 points; Germany 26; Italy 21
1968: USA 34 points; Gt. Britain 26; Italy and Germany 25
1969: Germany 39 points; Gt. Britain 35; Italy 29
1970: Gt. Britain 27½ points; Germany 25; Italy 15
1971: Germany 38 points; Gt. Britain 33; Italy 26
1972: Gt. Britain 33 points; Germany 32; Italy 20
1973: Gt. Britain 34 points; Germany 33; Switzerland 21
1974: Gt. Britain 37 points; Germany 33½; France 31
1975: Germany 39 points; Gt. Britain 35; Italy and Belgium 22
1976: Germany 32 points; France 31; Ireland 27
1977: Gt. Britain 35½ points; Germany 32, Ireland 31

Olympic Champions since 1920

Year Individual winner	Team winners
1920: Lt. T. Lequio (Italy) *Trebecco*	Sweden
1924: Lt. A. Gemuseus (Switzerland) *Lucette*	Sweden
1928: Capt. F. Ventura (Czechoslovakia) *Eliot*	Spain
1932: Lt. T. Nishi (Japan) *Uranus*	no team finished
1936: Lt. K. Hasse (Germany) *Tora*	Germany
1948: Col. H. Mariles (Mexico) *Arete*	Mexico
1952: P. J. d'Oriola (France) *Ali Baba*	Gt. Britain
1956: H.G. Winkler (Germany) *Halla*	Germany
1960: R. d'Inzeo (Italy) *Possillipo*	Germany
1964: P. J. d'Oriola (France) *Lutteur*	Germany
1968: W. Steinkraus (USA) *Snowbound*	Canada
1972: G. Mancinelli (Italy) *Ambassador*	Germany
1976: A. Schockemohle (Germany) *Warwick Rex*	France

159

Skating

Current champions in international ice-skating are as follows:

Olympic Championships, 1976
Figure-skating, men: J. Curry (Gt. Britain)
Figure-skating, women: D. Hammill (USA)
Pairs: A. Zaitsev, I. Rodnina (USSR)
Dance: G. Gorshkov, L. Pakhomova (USSR)
Sprint, men: E. Kulikov (USSR)
Sprint, women: S. Young (USA)

World Championships, 1978
Figure-skating, men: C. Tickner (USA)
Figure-skating, women: A. Poetsch (E. Germany)
Pairs: A. Zaitsev, I. Rodnina (USSR)
Dance: G. Karponosov, N. Linichuk (USSR)
Speed-skating, men: E. Heiden (USA)
Sprint, men: E. Heiden (USA)
Sprint, women: L. Sadchikova (USSR)

Swimming

Swimming is a sport in which girls in particular can reach the top at a very early age. Kornelia Ender, winner of four gold medals at the 1976 Olympic Games, was only 17 at the time.

World records, men

Event	Holder	Nation	Record	Year
100 m freestyle	J. Skinner	South Africa	49.44 s	1976
200 m freestyle	Bruce Furniss	USA	1 min 50.29 s	1976
400 m freestyle	Brian Goodell	USA	3 min 51.56 s	1977
1500 m freestyle	Brian Goodell	USA	15 min 02.40 s	1976
100 m backstroke	John Naber	USA	55.49 s	1976

200 m backstroke	John Naber	USA	1 min 59.19 s	1976
100 m breaststroke	G. Morken	W. Germany	1 min 02.86 s	1976
200 m breaststroke	David Wilkie	Gt. Britain	2 min 15.11 s	1976
100 m butterfly	Mark Spitz	USA	54.27 s	1972
200 m butterfly	Mike Bruner	USA	1 min 59.23 s	1976
400 m medley	Rod Strachan	USA	4 min 23.68 s	1976

World records, women

100 m freestyle	Kornelia Ender	E. Germany	55.65 s	1976
200 m freestyle	Kornelia Ender	E. Germany	1 min 59.26 s	1976
400 m freestyle	Petra Thumer	E. Germany	4 min 08.91 s	1977
800 m freestyle	Petra Thumer	E. Germany	8 min 35.04 s	1977
100 m backstroke	Ulricke Richter	E. Germany	1 min 01.51 s	1976
200 m backstroke	Birgit Treiber	E. Germany	2 min 12.47 s	1976
100 m breaststroke	Hannelore Anke	E. Germany	1 min 10.86 s	1976
200 m breaststroke	Marina Koshevaia	USSR	2 min 33.35 s	1976
100 m butterfly	C. Knacke	E. Germany	59.73 s	1977
200 m butterfly	Rosemarie Kother	E. Germany	2 min 11.22 s	1976
400 m medley	Ulricke Tauber	E. Germany	4 min 42.77 s	1976

161

Olympic Champions

The reigning Olympic swimming and diving champions (1976 Games) are as follows:

Men

100 m freestyle: Jim Montgomery (USA)
200 m freestyle: Bruce Furniss (USA)
400 m freestyle: Brian Goodell (USA)
1500 m freestyle: Brian Goodell (USA)
100 m backstroke: John Naber (USA)
200 m backstroke: John Naber (USA)
100 m breaststroke: John Hencken (USA)
200 m breaststroke: David Wilkie (Gt. Britain)
100 m butterfly: Matt Vogel (USA)
200 m butterfly: Mike Bruner (USA)
400 m medley: Rod Strachan (USA)
Springboard diving: Phil Boggs (USA)
Highboard diving: Klaus Dibiasi (Italy)

Women

100 m freestyle: Kornelia Ender (E. Germany)
200 m freestyle: Kornelia Ender (E. Germany)
400 m freestyle: Petra Thumer (E. Germany)
800 m freestyle: Petra Thumer (E. Germany)
100 m backstroke: Ulricke Richter (E. Germany)
200 m backstroke: Ulricke Richter (E. Germany)
100 m breaststroke: Hannelore Anke (E. Germany)
200 m breaststroke: Marina Koshevaia (USSR)
100 m butterfly: Kornelia Ender (E. Germany)
200 m butterfly: Andrea Pollak (E. Germany)
400 m medley: Ulricke Tauber (E. Germany)
Springboard diving: Jennifer Chandler (USA)
Highboard diving: Elena Vaytsekhovskaia (USSR)

162

Biographies of Sportsmen and Sportswomen

ALI, Muhammad. Ali changed his name from Cassius Clay when adopting the Muslim faith. Before that he was known as the 'Louisville Lip' because of his controversial utterances, in which he styled himself the 'Greatest'. Many good judges would agree with his assessment: he was certainly the greatest entertainer and most colourful character boxing has known. He won an Olympic Gold Medal as an amateur before taking the world heavyweight title from Sonny Liston when only 22 years old. He was a good champion, beating all logical challengers, until his refusal to join the U.S. Army forced him out of the ring for three years. He announced his retirement, but came back by popular demand, only to suffer eventually his first defeat at the hands of the new champion Joe Frazier. He was past his best, but he regained the championship from George Foreman in 1974. After losing it to Spinks in 1978, he became the first man to win the title three times by beating Spinks that same year. He has recently starred in a feature film about his own life.

BOARD, Lillian. The story of Lillian Board is one of sport's great tragedies. She was born in 1948 and first showed her potential at 18: when anchoring the Commonwealth 4 × 400 metres relay team in Los Angeles. In the 1968 Olympic Games she took the silver medal in the 400 metres. In 1969 she won gold medals in the European Championships at 800 metres and in the 4 × 400 metres relay, when in the final leg she overtook her Olympic Games conqueror, Colette Besson, to prove she was the best in the world. She was four times a member of a relay team which broke the world record, the last in 1970. Sadly, that year she died of cancer, a beautiful girl who was the darling of the fans with, apparently, gold medals waiting to be won. Her cheerfulness in her courageous fight against her illness is a poignant memory for all who followed her sports career.

BORG, Bjorn was born in 1956, and began to play tennis when he was eight years old, showing such promise that after four years he was spotted and coached by Lennart Bergelin. He was in Sweden's Davis Cup team when only 15, and at 18 was ranked fourth in the world. Initially, he attracted attention all round the world because of his style (he uses two hands for most of his ground shots and volleys) and the adoration he inspired in teenage girls. He often needed a police bodyguard. He won many championships before his triumph in the greatest, at Wimbledon in 1976. When he beat Jimmy Connors in five sets in the 1977 Wimbledon final he once again laid claim to being the best in the world, a claim he reinforced in 1978, when he again beat Connors in the final to become the first man to win Wimbledon three years running since Fred Perry 40 years before.

BRADLEY, Caroline joined the British show-jumping team in Dublin in 1966. She won on *Franco*, and was runner-up in the New York Grand Prix in 1967. She was second to Ann Moore in the European Championships in 1973 on *True Lass* and won puissance events in 1973 and 1974 on *New Yorker*, being the first lady to win the puissance at the Horse of the Year Show at Wembley. She turned professional in 1973.

BROOME, David was born in 1940 and has won several show jumping championships and trophies, as well as riding in four Olympic Games. He won an Olympic individual bronze medal in 1960 on *Sunsalve*, on whom he won the European Championship in 1961. On *Mister Softee* he had many successes including the King George V cup in 1966, the European Championships of 1967 and 1969, an Olympic bronze medal in 1968 and the British Jumping Derby at Hickstead. Having been third in the World Championship on *Sunsalve* in 1960, he had his greatest success in 1970, when he won on *Beethoven*. He turned professional in 1973, and his best horses since have been *Sportsman, Heatwave* and *Philco*. At the Wembley Horse of the Year Show in 1975 he won seven competitions. In 1977 he became the first rider to win the King George V Cup four times.

COMANECI, Nadia as a 14-year-old Rumanian gymnast, was undoubtedly the star of the 1976 Olympic Games. A year earlier she had won the combined exercises title and three individual apparatus events in the European Championships, overshadowing the great Russian gymnasts Ludmilla Touris-cheva, the previous Olympic champion, Nelli Kim, the new Russian No. 1, and Olga Korbut, who before Comaneci was the favourite of the spectators. In Montreal, Nadia excelled herself, six times being given the perfect score of ten for an exercise. She won gold medals on the asymmetric bars and beam, bronze on the floor exercises, and was fourth in the vault. She easily won the individual combined gold medal.

CONNORS, Jimmy was born in 1952 and his mother, a fully qualified coach, taught him to hit a tennis ball as soon as he could toddle. The family moved to California to get Jimmy the best coaching, and he won the All-America Inter-collegiate Championship. He turned professional in 1972 and became the biggest money-winner in the game. He seemed destined for a long reign as the world's No. 1 player when he won Wimbledon in 1974, easily beating Rosewall in the final. However, a supremacy, and when he lost to Borg in the 1977 and 1978 finals he had a genuine challenger for the title of world's best player.

CURRY, John. At Innsbruck in 1976 John Curry became the first British male skater to win an Olympic gold medal. Curry also won the World and European championships, and not only proved himself the best in the world, but altered skating values, making artistic expression as necessary as athleticism and technical excellence. From Birmingham, Curry trained at Richmond before going to the United States, where sponsor-ship by a wealthy American, coaching by one of the world's top coaches and unlimited access to ice helped him to the top. He is now a professional and has founded a theatre of skating.

ENDER, Kornelia proved herself the leading woman swim-mer of the world at the 1976 Olympic games where she won four gold medals. A product of the East German method of intensive training, she was recommended swimming lessons at the age of five to help cure hip pains. She was still not strong at 11 years

165

old when she was selected for special training, but systematic strengthening exercises built up the muscles that all who saw her Montreal successes on television will remember. She was still only 17 when she won her gold medals for the 100 and 200 metres freestyle, 100 metres butterfly and the 4 × 100 metres medley – new world records being set in each event.

EVERT, Chris was born four days before Christmas in 1954, the daughter of a tennis coach who was himself ranked 11th in the United States. She was very precocious as a player, beating Margaret Court, the world's No. 1, when she was only 15. Before she was 20, she was herself the world's leading player. Without a crushing service or smash, her supremacy is based on powerful ground strokes, clever placements and extreme steadiness. She turned professional in 1973, and quickly became the world's leading money-winner amongst the ladies. Miss Evert won the Wimbledon singles title in 1974 and 1976.

GILKS, Gillian. At the age of 24 Gillian Gilks was European and Commonwealth ladies singles champion in badminton, and Britain's Sportswoman of the Year. In 1976 she became All-England Champion, the title which was then unofficially recognised as the world champion. Born in 1950, she won the All-England Under-15 title when only twelve, and never looked back. Her impressive list of championships include singles, doubles and mixed doubles wins in the European, Commonwealth and All-England Championships and singles and doubles wins in the U.S. Open. In 1976 she was unbeatable, winning all championships open to her. Sadly, she was beaten in the final of the first official World Championships in 1977 and a dispute with the Badminton Association of Britain led to her missing the championships in 1978.

GORDON-WATSON, Mary is one of Britain's best three-day-event riders, and is associated mostly with her great horse *Cornishman V*. She was only 17 when *Cornishman V*, ridden by Richard Meade, helped Britain to win the gold medal at the 1968 Olympics. Mary rode him herself in 1969 to win the individual gold medal at the European Championships, and in 1970 the partnership won the World Championship. In the 1972 Olympics, Mary won a gold medal when Great Britain won the three-day event, finishing fourth on *Cornishman V* in the individual event. *Cornishman V* is now retired, and Mary is seeking his successor.

HUNT, James. In 1976 racing driver James Hunt won the World Championship, after the closest contest for years with Niki Lauda. Hunt, whose early days of racing earned him the nickname 'Hunt the Shunt' did his early Grand Prix racing with Hesketh Racing but switched to McLaren to win the title. When the Japanese Grand Prix, the last, began, Lauda was just ahead of Hunt, but Lauda's retirement meant that Hunt needed to finish fourth or better to win. He finished third, and followed fellow Britons Stewart, Clark, Hill, Surtees and Hawthorn as World Champion.

JOHNSEY, Debbie was selected for the British junior show jumping team when she was 11 years old, too young to compete in international events. Her first major successes were in 1973 when she won the Whitbread Young Riders title at Wembley and was Junior European Champion. Successes on *Moxy* in 1975 led to her selection for the 1976 Olympic team, where she was the youngest rider and only girl. She missed an Olympic silver medal by the narrowest of margins, finishing fourth after a jump-off which took place in torrential rain.

KEEGAN, Kevin is probably the most popular British soccer player still playing. He joined Liverpool in 1971 from Scunthorpe, and soon became the hero of the fans. He enjoyed six extremely successful seasons, winning medals for the League Championship, the FA Cup, and the UEFA Cup, ending in 1977 with a European Cup winners medal. Keegan had let it be known that at the end of the 1976–77 season he would like to play in Europe to enlarge his experience, and SV Hamburg beat other clubs by paying Liverpool nearly half a million pounds for his transfer.

KING, Billie-Jean was born in 1943 and first came into

prominence as a tennis-player as Miss Moffitt, winning the women's doubles championship at Wimbledon in 1961 and 1962. She remained at the top for longer than most modern women players, and last won the singles championships at Wimbledon in 1975. With Margaret Court, she dominated the women's game for over ten years, and has a splendid record at Wimbledon, winning six singles championships, nine women's doubles and four mixed doubles, a total of 19, equalling the record of Elizabeth Ryan, all of whose wins were in the doubles. She has been a great publicist for women's professional tennis, and in 1973 played a famous challenge match against Bobby Riggs, a pre-war Wimbledon champion, and won $100,000 by beating him before 30,000 spectators.

MACKEN, Eddie was born in 1950 and was already in the Irish show-jumping team when he began a brilliant association with *Pele* in 1974. He led the field for two days in the World Championship of that year, only to finish second to Hartwig Steenken. But he won the Wills Hickstead Gold Medal, and repeated his success in 1976. He turned professional in 1975 and was Europe's leading money winner in 1976, when he won the British Jumping Derby at Hickstead on *Boomerang*. In 1978, on *Boomerang*, he won the Aachen Grand Prix, and was second in the World Championship.

MOULD, Marion achieved fame as Marion Coakes when she won the Ladies' World Championship at show-jumping in 1965 at Hickstead. She was only 18 years old and she and her little horse *Stroller* became popular competitors at show-jumping events for many years. They won the Queen Elizabeth Cup in 1965 and 1971 and the British Jumping Derby at Hickstead in 1967, and helped Britain win the first President's Cup in 1965, when Marion was Sportswoman of the Year. From 1965 to 1969 they won the Wills Hickstead Gold Medal five years running, and they won an Olympic Silver Medal in the 1968 individual event. Marion, who married the Royal steeplechase jockey David Mould, is now looking for a successor to *Stroller*.

PETERS, Mary won fame at the 1972 Olympics in Munich, when she won the pentathlon, setting a world record. It was arguably the greatest athletic feat ever performed by a British sportswoman, and it won her, naturally, the Sportswoman of the Year Award. Mary was 33 years old at the time, and had been in athletics for a long time, first trying the pentathlon in 1956. The pentathlon in 1972 consisted of high jump, long jump and shot putt (which Mary won), 200 metres and 100 metres hurdles. Mary's total of 4,801 points was a new world record and is still the Olympic record.

PIGGOTT, Lester. Britain's greatest jockey since Gordon Richards, Lester Piggott is essentially a man for the big occasion, as his numerous Classic winners, including a record eight Derby winners, testifies. Piggott comes from a racing family, his father Keith having been a trainer and jockey, as were both his grandfathers, and he has uncles who won the Derby. Lester was riding at three years old, rode his first winner at 12 and his first Derby winner at 18. Piggott's main assets as a jockey are his strength and boldness, his dashing style often getting him into trouble in his younger days. The fight to keep his weight down has persuaded Piggott to cut down his number of rides in recent years, but he has been champion jockey nine times.

PRIOR-PALMER, Lucinda is one of Britain's leading three-day eventers. She won the 1973 Badminton Horse Trials on *Be Fair*. On the same horse she helped Britain win a bronze medal in the European Championships in Kiev in 1973 and a silver in Luhmuhlen in 1975, where she won the individual championship. Unfortunately *Be Fair* broke down in the 1976 Olympic Games after doing well in the dressage and cross-country, but Lucinda won at Badminton on her other good horse *Wide Awake,* and in 1977 won the European Individual Championship again on *George,* and helped Britain win the team championship.

SANDERSON, Tessa. In 1977 Tessa Sanderson, still

only 21, was Britain's leading girl athlete, and a doubly welcome champion since her event, throwing the javelin, is one in which Britain has lacked top quality performers. She raised the British record by a prodigious 10 metres, from 57.20m to 67.20m and had victories over three Olympic medallists and the future world record holder. In 1978 she won her first gold medal at the Commonwealth Games in Edmonton, and was second to the Olympic Gold medallist Ruth Fuchs in the European Championships. Born in 1956, Tessa still has her best years before her, and looks to be Britain's best prospect in field events for many years.

SMITH, Harvey is perhaps the best show-jumper not to have won an Olympic medal or major championship. He was second in the European Championships in 1967 and 1971 and third in the World Championship of 1970. He likes to dominate his horses, and his forceful personality shows in other directions. He has dabbled in all-in wrestling and even made a pop record. He has ridden many good horses, such as *O'Mally, Harvester, Madison Time, Mattie Brown, Summertime* and *Salvador*. He won the King George V Gold Cup in 1970 on *Mattie Brown,* and the British Jumping Derby in 1970 on the same horse and in 1974 on *Salvador*.

WADE, Virginia was born in 1945 and for many years has been Britain's leading women's tennis player. She has perhaps the best all-round game of all the women players, and sometimes has produced spells of breathtaking tennis, but except on a few notable occasions her nervousness at crucial times has prevented her from winning as often as she should. However, she won the first American Open Championship in 1968, and in 1977, Silver Jubilee Year, she delighted all her fans by winning, at last, the Wimbledon singles championship.

Louisa May Alcott (1832–88). An irresponsible father forced her to earn her own living from an early age. A dressmaking venture proved unsuccessful and she turned to writing stories for magazines. She became a nurse on the Unionist side in the American Civil War, and on her return home, began writing *Little Women* which met with instant success. This book, with its sequels, *Little Men* and *Good Wives*, has been loved by generations of children ever since.

Elizabeth Garrett Anderson (1836–1917) is remembered for her vigorous pioneering work campaigning for the right of women to enter the medical profession as doctors. By 1865, qualified but forbidden to practise, this remarkable woman obtained a diploma and became an apothecary. She opened a dispensary which, in time, became the New Hospital for Women. In 1870 she was, at last, appointed visiting physician to the East London Hospital.

Nancy, Viscountess Astor (1879–1964). American born, she succeeded her husband as M.P. for Plymouth in 1919 and was the first woman to take her seat in the House of Commons. Her pithy wit was often successfully matched against Winston Churchill, and she is especially remembered for her interest in social problems.

Jane Austen (1775–1817), one of the great English novelists. The daughter of a Hampshire clergyman, she was educated at home with her brothers. A charming and affectionate woman, she never married, although there is a hint of an affection for a young man who died suddenly. She began writing stories as a child, and four of her novels were published anonymously during her lifetime. *Pride and Prejudice, Persuasion* and *Emma* are probably the best loved.

Lilian Mary Baylis (1874–1937). After spending some time in South Africa, she returned to England in 1898, and helped with the management of the Royal Victoria Hall, which later became the Old Vic. In 1912, as manager, she introduced a programme of Shakespeare and opera. Run on a shoe-string, she somehow managed to keep the theatre open and, in 1931, she acquired Sadler's Wells Theatre for the exclusive presentation of opera and ballet.

Dorothea Beale (1831–1906), a pioneer of women's education. In 1858 she became principal of Cheltenham Ladies' College and, as a fighter for higher education for women, she sponsored St Hilda's Hall, Oxford. She is often remembered with Frances Mary Buss (1827–94) who founded the North London Collegiate School for Ladies.

Sarah Bernhardt (1844–1923), the greatest actress of her day, and still a theatrical legend. Born the daughter of a French magistrate and a milliner from Berlin, she trained at the Paris Conservatoire and made her debut in 1862, attracting little notice. Five years later, she won fame in Paris, and after 1876 she earned vast sums of money making frequent appearances in London, America and Europe. Married briefly to a Greek actor, she founded the Théâtre Sarah Bernhardt in 1899. In 1915, she had a leg amputated, but she did not abandon the stage.

Boadicea, Britain's warrior queen. In 60 AD, the Romans brutally took over the kingdom of the Iceni on the death of its king, Prasutagus, cruelly dispossessing his widow, Boadicea, and her daughters, of their birthright. In 61 AD, Boadicea, a woman of great courage, united the eastern tribes of Britain in revolt, while the Roman army was occupied in the west. After her initial successes, the Roman army was hurriedly brought back, and the undisciplined Britons were overwhelmingly defeated in the east midlands. Boadicea and her daughters committed suicide to evade capture.

Lucrezia Borgia (1480–1519) is known as one of the most infamous women in history, poisoning everyone who crossed her. Recent research has largely cleared her name, but this beautiful, intelligent woman was married off three times by her father, Pope Alexander VI, for political reasons. Her third

172

husband was the heir to the Duke of Ferrara and she used her power and his money to establish a brilliant court.

Charlotte Brontë (1816–55), one of the most gifted novelists of the nineteenth century. The daughter of an impoverished clergyman, she spent most of her life at Haworth, a village on the Yorkshire moors. At the age of eight she was sent away to Cowan's Bridge School, which became the Lowood of *Jane Eyre*. Her health broken, she returned to Haworth, where her father's austere and gloomy nature cast a shadow over his children's lives. From 1842–1844, she studied in Brussels with her sister Emily to equip herself as a governess. In one dreadful year, between 1848–1849, she lost her brother Branwell, and her two sisters, Emily and Anne. Left alone with her father in the bleak Haworth parsonage, she continued writing and, in 1852, she published *Villette*, her own favourite novel. After her father's death she married and died a year later in child-birth.

Elizabeth Barrett Browning (1806–61). Having injured her spine while trying to saddle her horse, Elizabeth Barrett led a retired life at her father's house in Wimpole Street, London. The shock of her brother's death in a boating accident at Torquay confined her for many years to her sickroom. In 1846, the poet Robert Browning first visited her, and the following autumn they were married. Living in Florence after her marriage, she is best remembered for her *Sonnets from the Portuguese*, a series of exquisite love poems.

Maria Meneghini Callas (1923–1977), the most outstanding operatic soprano of her age. Born in New York of Greek parents, she studied at the Athens Conservatory. From 1947 onwards she sang all the most exacting soprano roles. The memory of her wonderful voice and superb dramatic presence on stage will be treasured by everyone who heard her. She is, perhaps, best remembered for her interpretation of Tosca in Verdi's opera of the same name.

Julia Margaret Cameron (1815–79), a photographer of great distinction. Born at Calcutta, she married Charles Hay Cameron, the Indian jurist, in 1838. Her immense talent as a photographer is now recognised, and her portraits of Tennyson, Darwin, Carlyle, Newman – and other notables of her day – are now given the attention they deserve. She died, like her husband, in Ceylon.

Catharine the Great (1729–96), Empress of Russia. A German princess, she married Peter, the heir to the Russian throne in 1745. She soon quarrelled with her husband and began to take lovers. On Peter's accession in 1762, the couple's differences widened and they separated. Shortly afterwards, Peter was murdered, and Catharine became Empress, governing with great energy and increasing the power and dominions of Russia. Catharine introduced many western European ideas into her adopted country, and while she was a woman of great ability, she had a great many personal faults.

Edith Cavell (1865–1915), English heroine of World War I. The matron of a hospital in Brussels, she was executed by the Germans in 1915 for helping wounded Belgian and Allied prisoners to escape.

Christina, Queen of Sweden (1626–89). This beautiful and clever woman received a man's education and, in 1650, she was crowned with the title *king*. She grew weary of the restraints imposed upon her, and four years later abdicated in favour of her cousin. She became a Catholic, and entered Rome on horseback, dressed in the costume of an Amazon. On her cousin's death in 1660, she attempted to regain her throne, but this ended in failure. She died, something of an embarrassment to all concerned, in Rome.

Sarah Churchill, Duchess of Marlborough (1680–1744) – known as viceroy Sarah. A bosom friend of Princess Anne, the second daughter of James II, this spirited girl married John Churchill, an ambitious army officer who later became the great Duke of Marlborough. Advancing her husband's career while he was abroad, Sarah's influence became almost boundless on Anne's accession to the throne. She fell from power in 1711, supplanted by her cousin, Mrs Masham and, after her husband's death in 1722, lived in complete retirement. She died an immensely rich woman, leaving a fortune of £3,000,000.

Cleopatra (69–39BC). Deprived of her share in the throne of Egypt by her younger brother Ptolemy, she captivated Julius Caesar who restored her to her crown. After Caesar's murder, she was summoned by Mark Antony to appear before him, and his resulting infatuation lost him friends in Rome, and an army led by Octavian (later known as Augustus), marched against him. When Octavian arrived victorious at the gates of Alexandria, she tried to charm him, too. Finding that she could not touch him, she killed herself. Cleopatra was too proud to face the humiliation of being led captive through the streets of Rome at his triumph.

Emerald Cunard (1872–1948), was one of the last great society hostesses – an interesting figure of a bygone age. An American, she came to London in 1894, and as 'a necessary springboard to broader horizons', she married Sir Bache Cunard, the grandson of the founder of the shipping line. In 1911 she fell in love with Thomas Beecham and actively supported his crusade for English opera. Counting the Prince of Wales and Mrs Simpson among her many friends, she used her social position to raise money for the arts.

Marie Curie (1867–1934) – the only person to win two Nobel prizes. A Pole, Marie worked with her husband, Pierre, on magnetism and radio-activity in Paris. Finally, they discovered radium and shared a Nobel prize for their work. Three years later, Pierre was killed in a road accident. Marie succeeded to her husband's chair of Physics at the Sorbonne and carried on her research. In 1911, she was awarded a second Nobel prize for isolating radium and polonium. Just before her death, her daughter, Irène Joliot Curie, and her son-in-law, Professor Joliot, were awarded a Nobel prize for induced radio-activity.

Mary Baker Eddy (1821–1910), the founder of the Christian Science movement. An invalid for many years, established medicine did nothing for her and she decided to try spiritual and mental healing. Using the incident in St Matthew's Gospel, where a paralysed man got up and walked, she recovered. She founded the Church of Christ Scientist (1879) in Boston, and two years later was ordained minister.

George Eliot, the pen-name of Mary Ann Evans (1819–80), whose pictures of farmers and tradesmen are unsurpassed in English literature. The daughter of a Warwickshire land-agent who later turned farmer, she became deeply involved in the evangelical movement. On her father's death, she travelled extensively, and in 1854 she met G.H. Lewes and formed a liaison with him that lasted until his death in 1878. Her novels include *Adam Bede, The Mill on the Floss, Silas Marner* and *Middlemarch*, which is generally considered to be her greatest work.

Elizabeth Ist, arguably England's most brilliant queen. The daughter of Henry VIII and Anne Boleyn, she was brought up a Protestant and educated as a Renaissance princess. The centre of Protestant plots during the reign of her unpopular Catholic sister, Mary, Elizabeth knew great danger and learned to keep her own counsel, which served her well in later life. On her accession in 1558, she quickly showed her ability in surrounding herself with able ministers. Under her guidance, and in spite of the threat from Spain, England entered a golden age.

Dame Edith Evans (1888–1976), one of the greatest actresses of the English theatre. Throughout her long career, she played an enormous number of roles, although there are perhaps two which she made especially her own – that of Mrs Millament in *The Way of the World* and Lady Bracknell in *The Importance of Being Earnest*.

Kathleen Ferrier (1912–53). In 1940, she won a prize for singing at a local music festival. Her success led her to study seriously and the range and richness of her beautiful contralto voice, together with her remarkable technical control, rapidly won her a great reputation, which led to performances all over the world.

Elizabeth Fry (1780–1845). The daughter of a rich Quaker banker, she married Joseph Fry, a London merchant, in 1800. A visit to Newgate prison in 1813, and the appalling conditions she found there, made her decide to devote her life to prison reform both at home and abroad. She also founded shelters for the homeless and performed other charitable work – and all this in spite of her husband's bankruptcy (1828), and their fall from affluence to real poverty.

Mary Wollstonecraft Godwin (1759–97), the first advocate for the equality of the sexes. Daughter of a drunken ne'er-do-well, she was forced to earn her own living at the age of nineteen. In 1788, she became literary adviser to Johnson, the publisher, and this brought her into contact with the reformers of her day. She went to Paris, alone, during the winter of 1792, and witnessed the horrors of the French revolution. While she was there, she met an American, Gilbert Imlay, and bore him a daughter. A suicide attempt finally drove him away from her but, in 1797, she married the philosopher William Godwin. She died shortly after bearing him a daughter, Mary, who later became the wife of Shelley, the poet. This daughter was later to write *Frankenstein* while visiting Lord Byron with Shelley in the summer of 1816.

Constance Frederica Gordon-Cumming (1837–1924). Born at Altyre, Elginshire, she went to India at the invitation of friends. Her spritely and entertaining diaries record, in detail, the life she saw, and many of her fascinating watercolours still exist. Travelling alone with her native bearers, she forded rivers and climbed mountains in full Victorian dress. On her return from India, she travelled to the South Sea Islands, America, China and Ceylon, leaving behind invaluable documents of great social interest.

Emma Hamilton (1765–1815). After a colourful career, she became the mistress of the Hon. Charles Greville in 1782. By 1786, she had exchanged him for his uncle, Sir William Hamilton. They went to Naples together, and five years later they married. Nelson first met her in 1793 and their friendship changed into an enduring passion. However, this ill-assorted trio remained firm friends. After the deaths of Nelson and her husband, Emma found it impossible to live within her means, and she was arrested for debt in 1813. The following year, she fled to Calais and died in 1815.

Joan of Arc (1412–31), the Maid of Orleans. France was torn apart by the Hundred Years War, and this simple peasant girl's ardent prayers were answered by visions which convinced her that she was chosen by God to deliver her country. Eventually, she succeeded in persuading the Dauphin of her sincerity and, putting on white armour and with a force of some 400 men, she raised the seige of Orleans. Within six weeks in 1429, she swept the English from their principal positions on the river Loire. She stood beside the Dauphin at his coronation at Reims, but in 1430 she was captured by the Burgundians and sold to their English allies. She was tried at Rouen as a sorceress and heretic, and shameful brutality made this bewildered girl of nineteen renounce her visions. Condemned to perpetual imprisonment, she recanted and was burnt at the stake. In 1920, she was canonised a saint.

Amy Johnson (1903–41) caught the public imagination in 1930 when she became the first woman to make a solo flight from England to Australia. In the next two years, this intrepid airwoman made further record flights to India, Japan and South Africa. Her last flight took place in 1941. Her plane developed engine trouble over the Thames estuary; she bailed out and was never seen again.

Mary Kingsley (1862–1900). A niece of Charles Kingsley, the author of *The Water Babies* and *Westward Ho!*, this intrepid woman travelled extensively in West Africa. She died as a nurse in a South African Hospital during the Boer War.

Lady Caroline Lamb (1785–1828). An aristocrat, the daughter of the Earl of Bessborough, she married William Lamb, an aspiring politician, who later became Viscount Melbourne. Beautiful and strong-willed, she wrote some novels under her married name, but is best remembered for the scandal she caused by her notorious pursuit of Lord Byron, the darling of society.

Flora Macdonald (1722–90), Scottish heroine of the '45 rebellion. Although she was not a Jacobite, she is said to have helped in Bonnie Prince Charlie's escape from Scotland to France in June 1746. Her bravery aroused admiration among the English as well as the Scots, and she was much fêted during her subsequent captivity.

Maria Theresa (1717–80), Empress of Austria and Queen of Hungary. As the daughter of the Emperor Charles VI, she was debarred by Austrian law from accession to the throne. Her father tried to buy off the European powers with the 'Pragmatic Sanction', but this fell apart on his death, and it took two major European wars to confirm her right to the throne. A woman of undaunted spirit, her combination of tact and energy, and her real concern for the conditions of her peoples, won her their love and admiration. She raised Austria from a weak and exhausted state to a major European power.

Marie Antoinette (1755–93), the ill-fated queen of France. The fourth daughter of Maria Theresa of Austria, she was not educated for the position she was to fill as wife of the heir to the throne of France. Spoilt, strong-willed and beautiful, she soon wearied of the stiff etiquette of the French court. Extravagant to a degree, she became extremely unpopular. When she became Queen, her political judgement was misguided and she became the centre of opposition to new ideas. However, her dignity and bravery rose to the heroic during the terrible events of the French revolution, and the way she met her death has earned her the admiration and sympathy of later generations.

Mary, Queen of Scots, (1542–87), Scotland's tragic queen. Spoiled and pampered as a young girl, Mary lacked political judgement throughout her turbulent reign. Forced finally to escape from Scotland, she fled to her cousin, the English queen, Elizabeth. As the Catholic heir to the English throne, Elizabeth could not risk giving her liberty, and many years of imprisonment followed. At the centre of Catholic plots to usurp the English throne, Elizabeth was finally forced to bring her to trial. Sentenced to death, Mary died on February 8th, 1587.

Lady Mary Wortley Montagu (1689–1762), the only daughter of the Duke of Kingston. When her husband, Edward Wortley Montagu, obtained a commissionership at the Treasury, Lady Mary moved to London where she gained a brilliant reputation and became a friend of Addison, Pope and many others. Her husband was later appointed Ambassador at Constantinople, and it was from here that she introduced the idea of inoculation for smallpox into England, and wrote her entertaining *Letters*, describing Eastern life.

Florence Nightingale (1820–1910), one of the most famous woman of the nineteenth century. Trained in Germany and France, she left England with thirty-eight nurses on the outbreak of the Crimean War. She arrived at Scutari in time to receive the wounded from the battle of Inkermann, and soon had 10,000 men in her care. Appalling sanitary conditions accounted for the frightful mortality, and she devoted herself to their reform. At the end of the war, a fund of £50,000 enabled her to form a college of nursing at St Thomas's Hospital.

Emmeline Pankhurst (1857–1928). With her husband, she began to campaign for women's right to vote in 1880. In 1905, together with her daughters Sylvia and Christabel, she organised the Women's Social and Political Union. Disruptive methods brought attention to the cause, but male opposition prevented any headway. The advent of the First World War brought women into heavy industry and farming in numbers that had never been seen before, and after the war ended votes were granted to women over thirty. In 1928, the suffrage was extended to all women over the age of twenty-one.

Anna Pavlova (1885–1931), a legend of the ballet. Born in St Petersburg, of humble parents, her star quality was almost immediately recognised at the Russian Imperial Ballet School. Eventually she founded her own company, and took it all over the world. Her most admired roles were in Swan Lake, Giselle and the Californian Poppy.

Jean Antoinette Poisson, Marquise de Pompadour (1721–64). A woman of remarkable grace, beauty and wit, she was brought up by her mother to believe that the role of the king's favourite was the summit of feminine ambition. She eventually succeeded in catching Louis XV's eye at a ball, and was installed at Versailles. The court was scandalised because she was a bourgeoise and Louis gave her the title of Marquise de Pompadour. She held her position for twenty years until her death in 1764, and influenced French policy to disastrous effect.

Helena Rubenstein (1882–1965). Born of Polish parents, she went to Australia as a young girl and opened her first beauty salon in Sydney, where she taught Australian women to protect their skins against the hot, dry climate and the strong sun. Her success led to salons in London, Paris and New York. Her multi-million dollar cosmetic business is based on using natural ingredients in her products and her philosophy of total beauty for the body has influenced generations of women.

Madame de Staël (1776–1817), the only daughter of the French statesman, Necker. She was a woman of irresistible personality who shone in pre-revolutionary Paris, where her salon was justly famous. Exiled in England during the revolution, she was allowed to return to Paris by Napoleon. Her salon was more brilliant than ever, but it became a centre for dissidents and Napoleon eventually banished her. She set out for Weimar, where she dazzled the whole court and met Schiller and Goethe. In 1804, she travelled to Italy with Schlegel, Wilhelm von Humboldt and Bonstetten. Her most famous work, *D'Allemagne*, was published in London, and admiration for her reached its height.

Marie Stopes (1880–1958) is best known for her work as a pioneer of birth control. Her first marriage ended in failure, and in 1918 she published her book *Married Love* in which she mentioned birth control. A storm of controversy followed, and in 1921, she opened her first birth control clinic in North London.

Arabella Stuart (1575–1615), one of history's tragic women. Born with Tudor blood in her veins, she became the centre of a plot against James I on his accession to the English throne. She secretly married William Seymour in 1610. William had been suspected of being her lover in 1602, and the unhappy pair were imprisoned by the king. They both escaped; but, tragically, Arabella was recaptured and died insane in the Tower.

St Teresa of Avila (1515–82), Spanish mystic and reformer. A Carmelite nun, by 1555, her asceticism and sanctity had led to visions which indicated that she should reform her order. She wrote about her religious experiences in *The Way to Perfection*, *The Book of the Foundations*, and *The Interior Castle*.

Violette Szabo (1921–1945), one of the most daring English secret agents of the Second World War. The tragic death of her French husband in Libya led her to volunteer for service behind enemy lines in France, and her heroic exploits in the daring plan to stop crack German reinforcements being put into action after the D-Day landings were entirely successful. Eventually she was captured by the Germans and shot at the Ravensbruck Prison Camp in the closing stages of the war. She was posthumously awarded the George Cross for her gallantry, and her story is told in the book, *Carve Her Name With Pride*.

Victoria (1819–1901), Queen of the United Kingdom and Ireland and Empress of India. Her long life spanned one of the most exciting periods of English history, and she gave her name to the age. She ascended the throne when she was only eighteen and, in 1840, married Prince Albert of Saxe Coburg and Gotha. She became devoted to him, and his early death in 1861 led to her seclusion from public life for several years. Coaxed out of mourning by Disraeli, she played her part as Queen and brought her influence to bear on government policy.

Virginia Woolf (1882–1941), novelist and critic. This brilliant woman, who became one of the central figures of the Bloomsbury set, suffered from mental ill health all her life. Intellectual and emotional strain was liable to throw her into fits of suicidal despair and even the loving care of her writer husband, Leonard, did not save her, when under the strain of war she drowned herself in 1941. Her most famous books are *To the Lighthouse*, *The Waves*, and *Orlando*.

THE WORLD:
USEFUL FACTS AND FIGURES

These tables of sizes, distances, heights and depths, numbers and locations of various things in the world we live in should help in settling many school and family arguments.

The diagram below shows how far the planets are from the Sun in millions of miles and kilometres:

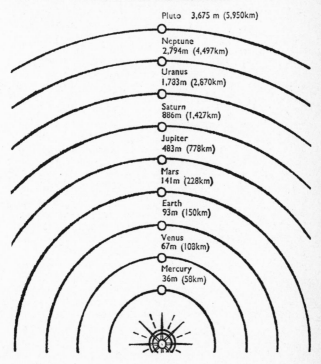

Pluto 3,675 m (5,950km)

Neptune
2,794m (4,497km)

Uranus
1,783m (2,870km)

Saturn
886m (1,427km)

Jupiter
483m (778km)

Mars
141m (228km)

Earth
93m (150km)

Venus
67m (108km)

Mercury
36m (58km)

The Solar System

The sun—the centre of our solar system—has a diameter of about 865,000 miles (1,392,000 km). The earth is one of nine planets which revolve round the sun. Here are these planets, together with some facts about them:

Planet	Diameter Miles	kilometres	One Revolution around Sun (days)	One Rotation on Axis
Mercury	3,008	4,840	88	88 days
Venus	7,600	12,300	225	not certain
Earth	7,927	12,756	365¼	23 h. 56 m.
Mars	4,200	6,790	687	24 h. 37 m.
Jupiter	88,439	134,700	4,332	9 h. 50 m.
Saturn	75,060	107,700	10,759	10 h. 14 m.
Uranus	30,875	47,100	30,687	10 h. 49 m.
Neptune	33,000	51,000	60,127	15 h. 40 m.
Pluto	3,600	5,900	90,400	unknown

The moon—the earth's satellite—has a diameter of 2,160 miles (3,476 km) and it is approximately 239,000 miles (385,000 km) away from the earth. Space flights to the moon have revealed no sign of life there, and no definite traces have been discovered on any of the planets—but studies point to possible life of some sort on Mars, probably in the vegetable category.

Land and Water

Much more than half the world's surface is ocean. In fact, the land area is only 55,786,000 square miles (143,500,000 square km) out of a total of 196,836,000 (508,500,000). The four great oceans are:

Name	Area (millions of sq. miles)	(millions of sq. km)
Pacific	64	165
Atlantic	31.5	81.5
Indian	28.35	73.5
Arctic	5.5	14.25

The six continents are:

Name	Area (millions of sq. miles)	(millions of sq. km)
Asia	17	44
Africa	11.7	30.3
North America	9	23.3
South America	7	18.1
Europe	3.8	9.8
Oceania	2.975	7.7

Ocean Deeps

Position	Name	Depth (feet)	(metres)
Mariana Trench	Challenger Deep	37,800	11,520
Tonga Trench	—	34,885	10,630
Philippine Trench	Galathea Deep	34,580	10,540
Kurile Trench	Vityaz Deep	34,045	10,375
Japanese Trench	Ramapo Deep	34,035	10,372
Kermadec Trench	—	32,788	9,995
Guam Trench	—	31,614	9,632
Puerto Rico Trench	Milwaukee Deep	30,246	9,200
New Britain Trench	Planet Deep	29,987	9,140

Great Seas and Lakes

Name and Location	Area (sq. miles)	(sq. km)
Mediterranean Sea (Southern Europe, Africa, Asia Minor)	1,100,000	2,850,000
South China Sea (China, East Indies)	960,000	2,486,000
Bering Sea (Alaska, Siberia)	878,000	2,274,000
Caribbean Sea (Central America, West Indies)	750,000	1,942,000
Gulf of Mexico (United States, Mexico)	716,000	1,855,000
Sea of Okhotsk (Siberia)	589,000	1,525,000
Hudson Bay (Canada)	475,000	1,230,000
Sea of Japan (Japan, U.S.S.R., Korea)	389,000	1,007,500
North Sea (North-western Europe)	221,000	572,400
Red Sea (Africa, Arabia)	178,000	461,000
Caspian Sea (U.S.S.R., Persia)	170,000	440,300
Black Sea (U.S.S.R., Turkey, Eastern Europe)	166,000	430,000
Baltic Sea (Scandinavia, U.S.S.R.)	163,000	422,000
Lake Superior (U.S.A., Canada)	31,820	82,400
Lake Victoria (East Central Africa)	26,820	69,480
Aral Sea (U.S.S.R.)	26,000	67,340
Lake Huron (U.S.A., Canada)	23,010	59,575
Lake Michigan (U.S.A.)	22,400	58,000
Lake Tanganyika (East Africa)	12,700	32,890

Large Islands

Name	Area (sq. miles)	(sq. km)
Greenland	840,000	2,175,600
New Guinea	345,000	893,500

186

Borneo	290,000	751,100
Madagascar	228,000	590,500
Baffin Land (Canada)	197,700	512,000
Sumatra	163,000	422,200
Great Britain	89,000	230,500
Honshu (Japan)	87,500	226,600
Ellesmere (Canada)	77,000	199,400
Celebes	72,500	187,800
South Island (New Zealand)	58,500	151,500
Java	48,400	125,400
North Island (New Zealand)	44,500	115,250
Cuba	44,000	114,000
Newfoundland (Canada)	42,750	110,700
Luzon (Philippine Islands)	41,000	106,200
Iceland	40,000	103,600

Great Rivers

Some of the longest rivers of the world are as follows:

River	Outflow	Length miles	kilometres
Nile	Mediterranean	4,160	6,695
Amazon	Atlantic	4,050	6,520
Missippi-Missouri-Red Rock	Gulf of Mexico	3,710	5,970
Yangtze	North Pacific	3,400	5,470
Yenisei	Arctic	3,300	5,310
Mekong	China Sea	2,800	4,500
Congo	Atlantic	2,710	4,375
Amur	North Pacific	2,700	4,345
Ob	Arctic	2,700	4,345
Lena	Arctic	2,680	4,310
Mackenzie	Beaufort Sea	2,635	4,240
Niger	Gulf of Guinea	2,600	4,185

Hwang-ho	North Pacific	2,600	4,185
Parana	Atlantic	2,450	3,940
Volga	Caspian Sea	2,290	3,685
Yukon	Bering Sea	1,979	3,185
St. Lawrence	Gulf of St. Lawrence	1,900	3,055
Rio Grande	Gulf of Mexico	1,885	3,035
São Francisco	Atlantic	1,800	2,895
Danube	Black Sea	1,770	2,850
Salween	Gulf of Martaban	1,700	2,735
Euphrates	Persian Gulf	1,700	2,735
Indus	Arabian Sea	1,700	2,735
Brahmaputra	Bay of Bengal	1,680	2,700
Zambezi	Indian Ocean	1,633	2,625

High Waterfalls

Some of the world's highest waterfalls (in a single leap) are as follows:

Falls	Country	Drop Feet	Metres
Angel	Venezuela	2,648	807
Cuquenan	Venezuela	2,000	610
Ribbon	U.S.A.	1,612	490
W. Mardalsfoss	Norway	1,535	467
Upper Yosemite	U.S.A.	1,430	436
Gavarnie	France	1,385	421
Tugela	South Africa	1,385	412
Glass	Brazil	1,325	403
Krimmi	Austria	1,250	381
Takkakaw	Canada	1,200	366
Silver Strand	U.S.A.	1.170	357

Geissbach	Switzerland	1,150	350
Wollomombie	Australia	1,100	335
Cusiana	Colombia	984	300
Staubbach	Switzerland	984	300
E. Mardalsfoss	Norway	974	297
Helena	New Zealand	890	271
Vetisfoss	Norway	889	271
Chirombo	Zambia	880	268

The famous Victoria Falls (Rhodesia, Zambia) has a drop of 355 feet (108 metres) and Niagara Falls (U.S.A., Canada) has a drop of 193 feet (59 metres).

Great Lakes

Some of the world's greatest lakes are as follows:

Lake	Location	Area Square miles	Square kilometres
Caspian Sea	Asia	170,000	440,300
Superior	North America	31,820	82,400
Victoria Nyanza	Africa	26,820	69,480
Aral	U.S.S.R.	26,000	67,340
Huron	North America	23,010	59,575
Michigan	North America	22,400	58,000
Tanganyika	Africa	12,700	32,890
Great Bear	Canada	12,200	31,600
Baikal	U.S.S.R.	12,150	31,470
Great Slave	Canada	11,170	28,930
Malawi	Africa	11,000	28,490
Erie	North America	9,940	25,740

Highest Mountains

Some of the World's highest mountains are as follows:

Mountain	Country	Height Feet	Metres
Everest	Nepal, Tibet	29,028	8,850
K2 (Godwin Austen)	Kashmir	28,250	8,610
Minya Konka	China	24,900	7,590
Aconcagna	Argentina	22,976	7,000
McKinley	Alaska	20,320	6,190
Logan	Canada	19,850	6,050
Kilimanjaro	Tanzania	19,340	5,890
Elbruz	U.S.S.R.	18,526	5,660
Mont Blanc	France	15,771	4,800
Ben Nevis	Scotland	4,406	1,340

Many other peaks in the Himalayas and Andes mountain ranges are nearly as high as Everest and Aconcagna but are not listed.

Natural Resources of the World

Meat and Dairy Produce. Most peoples of the world are meat eaters, and though cattle for meat can be raised on rough grassland, rich pasture is needed for dairy cattle, the source of milk, from which butter and cheese are made. The great beef-producing countries are the United States, Canada, Argentina and Australia. The major dairying nations are New Zealand, Australia, the United States, Denmark and the Netherlands.

Sheep and Wool Produce. The big sheep-producing countries are Australia, New Zealand, Argentina and Russia. The ideal sheep for economic breeding is a cross between the English strain, raised for its tender meat, and the Merino, of Mediterranean breed, noted for its wool and leather.

Cereals. Man has been developing cereals from the original wild grasses of the world since he first began to cultivate the soil. The principal cereals are wheat, oats, barley, rice, rye and maize. The great wheat areas of the world are Canada, the United States, Argentina, Australia and Eastern Europe. Asia is the source of most of the world's rice.

Tea. Tea is grown mainly in India, China, Ceylon and Japan, with the greatest export trade being carried out by India, which sends millions of pounds in weight every year to the major tea-drinking countries.

Coffee. The coffee plant, which takes five years to grow to a crop-yielding size, is grown mainly in Brazil, Colombia and East Africa.

Cocoa. The cocoa bean was brought back to Europe from Central America in the fifteenth century, by the first explorers. Today the principal growing area is West Africa, which produces enormous quantities every year for making chocolate and cocoa powder.

Sugar. There are two sources of sugar. These are sugar cane and sugar beet. Sugar cane is a tropical plant of which the stems yield a syrupy juice. This is boiled to purify and crystallise it. The juice of the sugar beet, a vegetable grown in temperate climates, is refined in a similar way. The principal sugar cane area is the West Indies.

Tobacco. Grown wild by the natives of North America, tobacco was brought to Europe in the sixteenth century. The main plantations are in the southern United States, but tobacco is also grown extensively in Rhodesia and the Middle East.

Cotton. Sub-tropical areas are best for cotton production, and the principal cotton countries are the United States, in its southern states, the West Indies, Egypt, India, China and southern Russia.

Rubber. Though some countries now produce much of their rubber by synthetic processes, rubber is still a major source of agricultural revenue for countries bordering the Equator. The main growing area embraces Malaysia, to which the original rubber trees were brought from Brazil, and nearby islands of Malaysia and Indonesia. Rubber is collected by cutting narrow grooves in the bark and allowing the natural rubber, or 'latex' to drip into a cup attached to the tree.

Minerals. Mineral ores are the source of the metals man needs, and most of them are found at considerable depth. Open-cast mining is used for surface lodes of minerals, but most mines are deep shafts with underground galleries penetrating hundreds of feet into the heart of the lode. Gold is found mainly in South Africa, Australia and North and South America. Copper and lead are found in every continent, silver in Central and South America and the Far East, and iron in most parts of the world. Uranium, the important metallic element used for atomic energy, is found mainly in the pitchblende deposits of the Congo and Canada.

Fuel. Coal, oil and natural gas are the fuels on which modern industrial society is based. Coal of varying quality is found in most parts of the world, and is extensively mined in Britain, Europe, the United States and the U.S.S.R. The great oil-producing countries are the United States, Canada, Venezuela and the Middle Eastern countries. Britain is expecting oil recently found in the North Sea to provide for much of her needs after 1980. Although only a small fraction of the world's oil and coal has been consumed, the demands of modern life are causing anxiety about when supplies will eventually run out. Nuclear power is already being produced, and other possible sources of energy being developed are the heat of the earth (geothermal energy) and the heat of the sun (solar energy).

Fisheries. Sea fishing is carried on in all parts of the world, but the areas which produce more than is needed for local consumption are the Grand Banks of Newfoundland, famous for cod, the herring fisheries of Iceland and those streching southward as far as the Portuguese coast, and the salmon areas of the North Pacific.

The World's Tallest Buldings

The highest buildings in England are:
Post Office Tower, London—580 ft (177 m)
Salisbury Cathedral (spire)—404 ft (123 m)
St. Paul's Cathedral (cross), London—365 ft (111 m)

The tallest tower in the world is at Ostankino, near Moscow, U.S.S.R. With its television antennae it reaches 1,762 feet (537 m). It has a 3-storey restaurant revolving near the top.

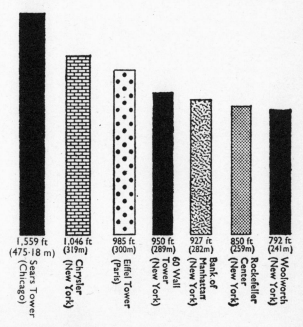

1,559 ft
(475·18 m)
Sears Tower
(Chicago)

1,046 ft
(319m)
Chrysler
(New York)

985 ft
(300m)
Eiffel Tower
(Paris)

950 ft
(289m)
60 Wall
Tower
(New York)

927 it
(282m)
Bank of
Manhattan
(New York)

850 ft
(259m)
Rockefeller
Center
(New York)

792 ft
(241m)
Woolworth
(New York)

The Seven Wonders of the World

It would be a hard task for anyone to name the Seven Wonders of the Modern World, but certainly among the candidates would be space travel, nuclear power, the jet engine, television, radar and some of the almost miraculous discoveries of recent years in medicine.

The Seven Wonders of the Ancient World were:

The Pyramids of Egypt, of which the biggest, the Great Pyramid of Cheops, was originally more than 480 feet (146 m) in height.

The Hanging Gardens of Babylon, near Baghdad. These were terraced gardens, irrigated by means of huge storage tanks on the uppermost terraces.

The Tomb of Mausolus at Halicarnassus, in Asia Minor.

The Temple of Diana (Artemis) at Ephesus, a great marble temple dating from c. 350 B.C.

The Statue of Jupiter (Zeus) at Olympia, built of marble and inlaid with gold about 430 B.C.

The Colossus of Rhodes, a bronze statue, about 105 feet (32 m) high, with its legs astride the harbour entrance at Rhodes.

The Pharos at Alexandria, the world's first real lighthouse.

Religions of the World

There remain well over 1,000 million of the world's population unclassified, because their religion is either unknown, or they have no religion, or because they follow primitive, tribal or other religions or beliefs.

Religions of the World

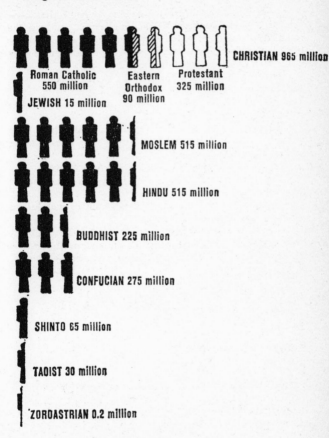

CHRISTIAN 965 million

Roman Catholic
550 million

Eastern
Orthodox
90 million

Protestant
325 million

JEWISH 15 million

MOSLEM 515 million

HINDU 515 million

BUDDHIST 225 million

CONFUCIAN 275 million

SHINTO 65 million

TAOIST 30 million

ZOROASTRIAN 0.2 million

195

Great Dates in History

B.C.

c. 3400	First Egyptian Dynastic Period
2900	The Great Pyramid of Egypt built by Cheops
1300	Phoenicians open up Mediterranean trade
1230	Exodus of the Israelites from Egypt
1190	Fall of Troy
961	Building of the Temple at Jerusalem begun
776	First Olympic Games held in Greece
753	Founding of Rome
490	Greeks defeat Persians at Marathon
488	Death of Buddha
335–23	The campaigns of Alexander the Great
146	Carthage destroyed by Scipio
55	Julius Caesar invades Britain
4	Actual date of the birth of Christ

A.D.

30	Crucifixion.
43	Conquest of Britain by Rome begun
70	Destruction of Jerusalem
79	Vesuvius erupts, destroying Pompeii and Herculaneum
122	Building of Hadrian's Wall
407	Romans leave Britain
476	Fall of the Roman Empire in the West
569	Birth of Mohammed in Mecca
711	Moors overrun Spain
732	Moors driven from France
1000	Norsemen reach Labrador
1066	Normans conquer Britain
1095	The Crusades begin
1215	The Magna Carta sealed by King John
1216	First Parliament in England
1271	Beginning of Marco Polo's travels
1338	Hundred Years War begins

1348	The Black Death sweeps Europe
1440	Printing with movable type begun in Germany
1453	Eastern Roman Empire falls to Turks
1455–85	Wars of the Roses
1476	First printing press in England
1492	Columbus discovers America
1492	Moors driven from Spain
1500	Portuguese discover Brazil
1519–22	First voyage round the world, by Magellan
1534	Reformation in England
1536	Dissolution of the monasteries in England
1572	Massacre of St. Bartholomew in France
1577–80	Drake's voyage round the world
1588	Drake defeats Spanish Armada
1605	Gunpowder Plot to blow up English Parliament
1607	First permanent colony established in Virginia
1618–48	Thirty Years War
1620	*Mayflower* colonists land in New England
1642	New Zealand and Tasmania discovered
1665	Great Plague of London
1666	Great Fire of London
1707	Act of Union unites England and Scotland
1715	First Jacobite Rebellion
1745	Second Jacobite Rebellion, 'The Forty-five'
1756	Beginning of Seven Years War
1760	British defeat French in Canada
1760	Beginning of Industrial Revolution
1770	Captain Cook discovers New South Wales
1775–83	American War of Independence
1776	American Declaration of Independence
1789	French Revolution begins
1796	Napoleonic Wars begin
1804	Napoleon becomes Emperor of France
1805	Battle of Trafalgar
1815	Battle of Waterloo
1832	First Reform Act in Parliament

1833	Britain abolishes slavery
1840	Introduction of penny post in Britain
1848	Gold discovered in California
1854–56	Crimean War
1857	Indian Mutiny
1861–65	American Civil War
1863	United States abolishes slavery
1867	Dominion of Canada established
1869	Suez Canal opens
1870–71	Franco-Prussian War
1877–78	Russo-Turkish War breaks power of Turkey in Europe
1899–02	Boer War
1903	First successful aeroplane flight, by Wright brothers
1904–05	Russo-Japanese War
1909	Blériot makes first cross-Channel flight
1909	Peary reaches North Pole
1911	Amundsen reaches South Pole
1912	Ocean liner *Titanic* sinks, 1,513 lost
1914	World War I begins
1915	Ocean liner *Lusitania* torpedoed, 1,500 lost
1917	United States enters World War I
1917	Russian Revolution
1918	End of World War I
1919	Alcock and Brown make first non-stop trans-Atlantic flight
1920	First meeting of League of Nations
1922	Mussolini marches on Rome
1924	Death of Lenin
1926	General Strike takes place in Britain
1927	Lindbergh makes first solo flight across Atlantic
1929	Start of the Great Slump
1931	Japan occupies Manchuria
1933	Hitler attains power in Germany
1935	Italy invades Ethiopia

1936–39	Civil War in Spain
1937	Japan begins war on China
1938	Germany annexes Austria, Munich Agreement
1939	Outbreak of World War II
1940	Germany invades Denmark, Norway, Netherlands, Belgium and Luxembourg
1940	Dunkirk evacuation. Paris taken by Germans
1940	Battle of Britain
1941	Russia and United States enter World War II
1942	All of France occupied by Germans
1943	Russians halt German advance at Stalingrad
1943	Allies invade Italy
1944	Allies invade France
1945	Germany surrenders. Hitler dies
1945	First atomic bomb dropped on Japan
1945	End of World War II
1945	Japan surrenders
1945	United Nations established
1947	India attains independence
1948	State of Israel proclaimed
1950–53	Korean War
1953	Conquest of Mount Everest
1956	Suez Canal dispute
1957	Russians launch first space satellites
1959	Russians launch first rocket to reach moon and photograph its far side
1960	Piccard descends 7 miles under the Pacific
1961	First space flight, by Yuri Gagarin
1963	Assassination of President Kennedy
1964	Pope Paul VI visits the Holy Land and becomes first reigning Pope to travel by air
1965	Death of Sir Winston Churchill
1966	River Arno overflows and floods two-thirds of the City of Florence, Italy
1967	China explodes complete H-bomb
1969	Neil Amstrong first man on the moon

1971	Indo-Pakistan conflict. East Pakistan becomes Bangladesh
1971	China admitted to the United Nations
1974	President Nixon resigns after impeachment proceedings
1975	End of Vietnam War

Exploration and Discoveries of the Past Years

1497	East coast of Canada, by John Cabot
1498	Cape route to India, by Vasco da Gama
1498	South America, by Christopher Columbus
1513	Pacific Ocean, by Vasco Nuñez de Balboa
1519	Magellan Strait, by Ferdinand Magellan
1534	St. Lawrence River, by Jacques Cartier
1605–06	Australia, by Willem Jansz
1610	Hudson Bay (Canada), by Henry Hudson
1616	Baffin Bay (Canada), by William Baffin
1642	New Zealand and Tasmania, by Abel Janszoon Tasman
1778	Hawaii, by James Cook
1820	Antarctic mainland, by Edward Bransfield
1855	Victoria Falls, by David Livingstone
1858	Source of the Nile, by John Hanning Speke
1865	Matterhorn summit first reached, by Edward Whymper
1909	North Pole first reached, by Robert E. Peary
1911	South Pole first reached, by Roald Amundsen
1958	American atomic-powered submarine *Nautilus* makes first undersea crossing beneath the North Pole ice cap in 96 hours
1965	Alexei Leonov becomes the first man to walk in space
1966	Russian Space probe achieves first soft landing on the Moon
1969	Neil Armstrong and Edwin Aldrin become the first men to land on the Moon

1971	American astronauts drive the 'Lunar Rover' across the Moon's Surface.
1972	America launches *Skylab*, an experimental space station.
1975	Russian *Soyuz* and American *Apollo* spacecraft successfully dock in space.
1976	American spacecraft, *Vikings I* and *II*, land on Mars.
1977	Space shuttle tests successfully carried out which are planned to come into operation in 1979.

The United Nations

The first full meeting of the United Nations was held in 1945, at San Francisco, and the building of the present headquarters, in New York, was begun soon afterwards. The 147 members of the United Nations are:

Afghanistan
Albania
Algeria
Angola
Argentina
Australia
Austria
Bahamas
Bahrain
Bangladesh
Barbados
Belgium
Benin
Bhutan
Bolivia
Botswana
Brazil
Bulgaria
Burma
Burundi

Byelorussian S.S.R.
Cambodia
Cameroon
Canada
Cape Verde
Central African
  Empire
Chad
Chile
China
Colombia
Comoros
Congo
Costa Rica
Cuba
Cyprus
Czechoslovakia
Denmark
Dominican Rep.
Ecuador

Egypt
Equatorial Guinea
Ethiopia
Fiji
Finland
France
Gabon
Gambia
Germany (East)
Germany (West)
Ghana
Greece
Grenada
Guatemala
Guinea
Guinea Bissau
Guyana
Haiti
Honduras
Hungary

Iceland
India
Indonesia
Iran
Iraq
Irish Republic
Israel
Italy
Ivory Coast
Jamaica
Japan
Jordan
Kampuchea
Kenya
Kuwait
Laos
Lebanon
Lesotho
Liberia
Libya
Luxembourg
Madagascar
Malawi
Malaysia
Maldive
   Islands
Mali
Malta
Mauritania
Mauritius
Mexico
Mongolian P.R.
Morocco
Mozambique
Nepal
Netherlands
New Zealand

Nicaragua
Niger
Nigeria
Norway
Oman
Pakistan
Panama
Papua New Guinea
Paraguay
Peru
Philippines
Poland
Portugal
Qatar
Romania
Rwanda
(El) Salvador
Sao Tomé
and Principe
Saudi Arabia
Senegal
Seychelles
Sierra Leone
Singapore
Somalia
South Africa
Spain
Sri Lanka
Sudan
Surinam
Swaziland
Sweden
Syria
Tanzania
Thailand
Togo
Trinidad and

Tobago
Tunisia
Turkey
Uganda
Ukraine
U.S.S.R.
United Arab
   Emirates
United Kingdom
United States
Upper Volta
Uruguay
Venezuela
Yemen
Yemen (P.D.R.)
Yugoslavia
Zaire
Zambia

The General Assembly consists of all members. Any important issue brought before it is settled by a two-thirds majority vote; lesser issues require only a simple majority. The Security Council is made up of fifteen members and is in continuous session to prevent international disputes. There are five permanent members: United Kingdom, United States, U.S.S.R., France and China. The General Assembly chooses the remaining members, electing them for a period of two years. The Council reaches procedure decisions by an affirmative vote of nine members, but in other matters five of the votes must be those of the permanent members. If any one of these members votes against the majority, this vote is in effect a veto, and no settlement can be reached.

There are four other sections of the United Nations: the Economic and Social Council, the Trusteeship Council, the International Court of Justice and the Secretariat.

The United Nations also runs various agencies. These are as follows: International Atomic Energy Agency (I.A.E.A.), International Labour Organization (I.L.O.), Food and Agriculture Organization of the United Nations (F.A.O.), United Nations Educational Scientific and Cultural Organization (U.N.E.S.C.O.), World Health Organization (W.H.O.), International Monetary Fund, International Bank for Reconstruction and Development (The World Bank), International Finance Corporation (I.F.C.), International Civil Aviation Organization (I.C.A.O.), International Telecommunication Union (I.T.U.), World Meteorological Organization (W.M.O.), Inter-governmental Maritime Consultative Organization (I.M.C.O.), General Agreement on Tariffs and Trade (G.A.T.T.).

Monarchs of the World

Almost all countries of the world today have a parliamentary system—that is, a council of people elected to rule.

By far the majority of nations have at their head a President, in most cases elected every few years. Those which still have hereditary monarchs are:

Country	Ruler	Came to Throne
Belgium	King Baudouin	1951
Denmark	Queen Margrethe II	1972
Great Britain	Queen Elizabeth II	1952
Iran	Shah Mohammed Reza Pahlevi	1941
Japan	Emperor Hirohito	1926
Jordan	King Hussein	1952
Liechtenstein	Prince Francis Joseph II	1938
Luxembourg	Grand Duke Jean	1964
Monaco	Prince Rainier III	1949
Morocco	King Hassàn II	1961
Nepal	Maharajadhiraja Birendra Bir Bikram Shah Dev	1972
Netherlands	Queen Juliana	1948
Norway	King Olav V	1957
Saudi Arabia	King Khaled ibn Abdul Aziz	1975
Spain	King Juan Carlos I	1975
Sweden	King Carl Gustaf	1973
Thailand	King Bhumibol Adulaydej	1946

The British Commonwealth of Nations

This is a free and equal association of the following nations: The United Kingdom, Australia, Bangladesh, Bahamas, Barbados, Bermuda, Botswana, British Honduras, Brunei, Canada, Cayman, Turks and Caicos Islands, Cyprus, Falkland Islands, Fiji, Gambia, Ghana, Gibraltar, Gilbert and Ellice Islands, Guyana, Hong Kong, India, Jamaica, Kenya, Lesotho, Malawi, Malaysia, Malta, Mauritius, Nauru, New Hebrides, New Zealand, Nigeria, Pitcairn, St Helena, Seychelles, Sierra Leone, Singapore, Solomon Islands, Sri

Lanka, Swaziland, Tanzania, Tonga, Trinidad and Tobago, Uganda, Western Samoa, Zambia, Rhodesia. The Queen is Head of the Commonwealth but only remains Head of State in certain instances.

The Royal Family

Her Majesty Queen Elizabeth II succeeded her father, King George VI, at his death on February 6, 1952. Her Coronation was on June 2, 1953. She was born on April 21, 1926, and on November 20, 1947, she married Prince Philip, son of Prince Andrew of Greece. Prince Philip, Duke of Edinburgh, was born on June 10, 1921. Their eldest son, Prince Charles Philip Arthur George, Prince of Wales, the heir to the Throne, was born on November 14, 1948. Their daughter, Princess Anne Elizabeth Alice Louise, was born on August 15, 1950, and on November 14, 1973, was married to Capt. Mark Anthony Peter Phillips, C.V.O., and has one son, Peter Mark Andrew, born on November 15, 1977. Their second son, Prince Andrew Albert Christian Edward, was born on February 19, 1960. Their third son, Prince Edward Antony Richard Louis, was born on March 10, 1964.

The other immediate members of the Royal Family are: Queen Elizabeth the Queen Mother, born August 4, 1900, widow of the late King George VI; Princess Margaret Rose sister of the Queen, born August 21, 1930.

The initial order of succession to the throne is: The Prince of Wales; Prince Andrew; Prince Edward; Princess Anne and her son; Princess Margaret and her son and daughter;

Kings and Queens of England

Name	Born	Reign	
Saxons and Danes		*From*	*To*
Egbert	*c.* 775	827	839
Ethelwulf	—	839	858

Ethelbald		—	858	860
Ethelbert		—	860	866
Ethelred I		—	866	871
Alfred the Great	c.	849	871	900
Edward the Elder	c.	870	900	924
Athelstan	c.	895	924	940
Edmund I	c.	921	940	946
Edred	c.	925	946	955
Edwy	c.	943	955	959
Edgar		944	959	975
Edward the Martyr	c.	963	975	978
Ethelred II, the Unready	c.	968	978	1016
Edmund II, Ironside	c.	980	1016	1016
Canute		994	1017	1035
Harold I	c.	1016	1035	1040
Hardicanute	c.	1018	1040	1042
Edward the Confessor	c.	1004	1042	1066
Harold II	c.	1020	1066	1066

House of Normandy

William I	1027	1066	1087
William II	1057	1087	1100
Henry I	1068	1100	1135
Stephen, Count of Blois	1104	1135	1154

House of Plantagenet

Henry II	1133	1154	1189
Richard I	1157	1189	1199
John	1166	1199	1216
Henry III	1207	1216	1272
Edward I	1239	1272	1307
Edward II	1284	1307	1327
Edward III	1312	1327	1377
Richard II	1367	1377	1399
Henry IV ⎫	1366	1399	1413
Henry V ⎬ *Lancaster*	1388	1413	1422
Henry VI ⎭	1421	1422	1461

Edward IV		1442	1461	1483
Edward V } *York*		1470	1483	1483
Richard III		1452	1483	1485

House of Tudor

Henry VII	1457	1485	1509
Henry VIII	1491	1509	1547
Edward VI	1537	1547	1553
Jane (Lady Jane Grey)—9 days	1537	1553	1553
Mary I	1516	1553	1558
Elizabeth I	1533	1558	1603

House of Stuart

James I (VI of Scotland)	1566	1603	1625
Charles I	1600	1625	1649

Commonwealth created May 19, 1649, causing Interregnum

Oliver Cromwell (Lord Protector)	1599	1653	1658
Richard Cromwell (Lord Protector)	1626	1658	1659

House of Stuart (Restoration)

Charles II	1630	1660	1685
James II	1633	1685	1688
William III } *joint sovereigns*	1650	1689	1702
Mary II	1662		1694
Anne	1665	1702	1714

House of Hanover

George I	1660	1714	1727
George II	1683	1727	1760
George III	1738	1760	1820
George IV	1762	1820	1830
William IV	1765	1830	1837
Victoria	1819	1837	1901

House of Saxe-Coburg

Edward VII	1841	1901	1910

House of Windsor

George V	1865	1910	1936
Edward VIII—325 days	1894	1936	1936
George VI	1895	1936	1952
Elizabeth II	1926	1952	—

Kings and Queens of Scotland

Name	**Reign**	
	From	*To*
Malcolm III (Canmore)	1057	1093
Donald I	1093	1094
Duncan II	1094	1094
Donald I (restored)	1094	1097
Edgar	1097	1107
Alexander I	1107	1124
David I	1124	1153
Malcolm IV (the Maiden)	1153	1165
William I (the Lion)	1165	1214
Alexander II	1214	1249
Alexander III	1249	1286
Margaret (Maid of Norway)	1286	1290
John Baliol	1292	1296
Robert I (Bruce)	1306	1329
David II	1329	1371
Robert II (Stewart)	1371	1390
Robert III	1390	1406
James I	1406	1437
James II	1437	1460
James III	1460	1488
James IV	1488	1513
James V	1513	1542
Mary (Queen of Scots)	1542	1587
James VI (became James I of England in 1603)	1567	1625

Britain's Prime Ministers and changes of administration

Date	Name	Party
1721	Sir Robert Walpole	Whig
1742	Earl of Wilmington	Whig
1743	Henry Pelham	Whig
1754	Duke of Newcastle	Whig
1756	Duke of Devonshire	Whig
1757	Duke of Newcastle	Whig
1761	Earl of Bute	Tory
1763	George Grenville	Whig
1765	Marquess of Rockingham	Whig
1766	Earl of Chatham	Whig
1767	Duke of Grafton	Whig
1770	Lord North	Tory
1782	Marquess of Rockingham	Whig
1782	Earl of Shelburne	Whig
1783	Duke of Portland	Coalition
1783	William Pitt	Tory
1801	Henry Addington	Tory
1804	William Pitt	Tory
1806	Lord Grenville	Whig
1807	Duke of Portland	Tory
1809	Spender Perceval	Tory
1812	Earl of Liverpool	Tory
1827	George Canning	Tory
1827	Viscount Goderich	Tory
1828	Duke of Wellington	Tory
1830	Earl Grey	Whig
1834	Viscount Melbourne	Whig
1834	Sir Robert Peel	Tory
1835	Viscount Melbourne	Whig
1841	Sir Robert Peel	Tory
1846	Lord John Russell	Whig

1852	Earl of Derby	Tory
1852	Earl of Aberdeen	Peelite
1855	Viscount Palmerston	Liberal
1858	Earl of Derby	Conservative
1859	Viscount Palmerston	Liberal
1865	Lord John Russell	Liberal
1866	Earl of Derby	Conservative
1868	Benjamin Disraeli	Conservative
1868	William E. Gladstone	Liberal
1874	Benjamin Disraeli	Conservative
1880	William E. Gladstone	Liberal
1885	Marquess of Salisbury	Conservative
1886	William E. Gladstone	Liberal
1886	Marquess of Salisbury	Conservative
1892	William E. Gladstone	Liberal
1894	Earl of Rosebery	Liberal
1895	Marquess of Salisbury	Conservative
1902	A. J. Balfour	Conservative
1905	Sir H. Campbell-Bannerman	Liberal
1908	Herbert Asquith	Liberal
1915	Herbert Asquith	Coalition
1916	David Lloyd George	Coalition
1922	Andrew Bonar Law	Conservative
1923	Stanley Baldwin	Conservative
1924	J. Ramsay MacDonald	Labour
1924	Stanley Baldwin	Conservative
1929	J. Ramsay MacDonald	Labour
1931	J. Ramsay MacDonald	Coalition
1935	Stanley Baldwin	Coalition
1937	Neville Chamberlain	Coalition
1940	Winston Churchill	Coalition
1945	Clement R. Attlee	Labour
1951	Sir Winston Churchill	Conservative
1955	Sir Anthony Eden	Conservative
1957	Harold Macmillan	Conservative
1963	Sir Alec Douglas-Home	Conservative

1964	Harold Wilson	Labour
1970	Edward Heath	Conservative
1974	Harold Wilson	Labour
1976	James Callaghan	Labour

How Laws are Made and Who Makes Them

New laws are discussed and voted upon in the two Houses of Parliament. The House of Lords, presided over by the Lord High Chancellor, has a membership of about one thousand, comprising Royal princes, archbishops, dukes, marquesses, earls, viscounts, bishops, barons, life peers and law lords. The House of Commons, directed by the Speaker, is an elected assembly of 635 men and women (previously 630) who are paid an annual salary for attendance. Each represents a constituency (area of the country) which elected him or her by majority vote at the last General Election, or a later By-election caused by the death or retirement of the previous representative. The normal span of a Parliament is five years, though at any time the Queen may, upon the advice of the Prime Minister, dissolve Parliament and proclaim a General Election. It is also possible that the Government may be defeated in the House of Commons on a major issue. It may then be forced to resign, in which case either the next strongest party forms a government, or a new election is sought. All but a handful of the Members of the House of Commons belong to one or other of the main political parties, and after a General Election it is the party with most Members which forms the Government. At certain times of national crisis, two or more parties may unite to form a Coalition Government.

New Laws start as Bills. Any Member of the Lords or Commons can introduce a Bill, though the majority are brought in by the Government, based on its plans as outlined in the Queen's Speech at the Opening of Parliament. The

211

Bill has to pass through three Readings before it is considered to be agreed by the House of Commons. It then goes forward to the House of Lords. If it is a Financial Bill, the House of Lords must pass it without making any changes, but the Lords can reject any other Bill; after the lapse of a year, the Lords' rejection does not prevent its being passed and forwarded to the Queen for her Assent.

General Elections—Results

Party	Votes	Seats in the House of Commons
1970		
Conservative*	13,144,692	330
Labour	12,179,166	287
Liberal	2,177,638	6
Others	903,311	7
* and associated parties		
1974 (Feb)		
Labour	11,654,726	301
Conservative	11,963,207	296
Liberal	6,063,470	14
Others	1,651,823	24
1974 (Oct)		
Labour	11,446,671	319
Conservatiue	10,445,951	276
Liberal	5,234,399	11
Communist	17,426	—
Plaid Cymru and Scottish Nationalist	982,172	13
Others	885,465	13

Speed Records

Fastest-ever by man. Space travel has provided the fastest means by which humans have travelled. The three fastest men were passengers in the Command Module of Apollo X in May 1969 – Col. Thomas P. Stafford, Cdr. E.A. Cernan and Cdr. J.W. Young. The speed reached was 24,791 mph (39,897 km/h).
Fastest-ever woman. Also an astronaut. In June 1963, Jnr. Lt. Valentina Vladimirovna Tereshkova-Nikolayev, in the spacecraft Vostok VI, travelled at 17,470 mph (28,115 km/h).
Fastest on land. Gary Gubelich achieved 627.287 mph (1,011 km/h) on October 23rd, 1970. He was driving a rocket-engined car called *The Blue Flame* on the Bonneville Salt Flats at Utah, USA. At one stage the car exceeded 650 mph (1,046 km/h).
Fastest woman on land. Mrs Kitty Hambleton in the rocket-engined three-wheeled *Motivator* recorded 512.710 mph (825 km/h) over the Alvard Desert, Oregon, USA in 1976. During the run she probably reached 600 mph (965 km/h).
Fastest woman in an aeroplane. Svetlana Savitskaya of Russia was reported to have flown at 1,669 mph (2,687 km/h) in 1975.
Fastest on water. Lee Taylor, Jnr. averaged 285.213 mph (459 km/h) over two 1-mile runs in the hydroplane *Hustler* on Lake Guntersville, Alabama, in 1967. The record for a propeller-driven craft is 202.42 mph (326 km/h) by Larry Hill. Donald Campbell reached 328 mph (528 km/h) on his fatal run in *Bluebird* on Coniston Water in 1967.
Speeds unassisted by machinery. The fastest speed attained by a jockey on a horse over a full 5-furlong race is nearly 42 mph (68 km/h). The fastest speed by a champion male swimmer (50 seconds for 100 metres) is only about 4.47 mph (7.18 km/h), and the fastest woman swimmer has managed 4.07 mph (6.45 km/h). The fastest male runners (10 seconds for 100 metres) travel at 22.37 mph (36 km/h) and the fastest women (11 seconds for 100 metres) at 20.34 mph (32.73 km/h).

Notable Bridges of the World

The world's longest bridge spans by type are as follows:

Suspension: Verrazano-Narrows Bridge, New York, built 1964. Length: 4,260 feet (1,298 metres).
Cantilever: Quebec Railway Bridge, Quebec, built 1917. Length: 1,800 feet (549 metres).
Steel Arch: Bayonne Bridge, New York, built 1931. Length: 1,652 feet (504 metres).
Covered Bridge: Hartland, New Brunswick. Length: 1,282 feet (391 metres).
Concrete Arch: Gladesville, Sydney, built 1964. Length: 1,000 feet (305 metres).
Stone Arch: Plauen, East Germany, built 1903. Length: 295 feet (90 metres).

The longest bridge span in Great Britain is the Firth of Forth road bridge, built in 1964, which has a main span of 3,300 feet (1,006 metres).

The world's longest railway bridge (built 1935) is the Huey P. Long Bridge in Louisiana, which carries the railway 4.35 miles (7 km). Its longest span is 790 feet (240 metres).

The world's highest bridge (built 1929) is over the Arkansas River in Colorado, and is 1,053 feet (321 metres) above the water level. The world's longest viaduct (road-carrying bridge) is the Second Lake Ponchartrain Causeway (built 1969) in Louisiana and is 23.87 miles (38.42 km) long.

The world's longest aqueduct (water-carrying bridge) is the California Aqueduct (built 1974) which is 444 miles (715 km) long. The longest aqueduct in Great Britain is the Pontcysyllte Aqueduct carrying the Shropshire Union Canal over the River Dee. Built in 1803 it is 1,007 feet (306 metres) long and 121 feet (37 metres) high.

214

Distances by Air

These are the distances of principal world cities from London by air, using the shortest routes.

Name	Distance (miles)	(km)	Name	Distance (miles)	(km)
Aden	4,104	6,604	Melbourne	11,934	19,206
Amsterdam	231	372	Montreal	3,310	5,327
Athens	1,501	2,416	Moscow	1,549	2,493
Baghdad	3,063	4,929	Munich	588	946
Berlin	593	954	Nairobi	4,429	7,128
Bombay	4,901	7,887	New York	3,500	5,633
Brussels	218	351	Nicosia	2,028	3,264
Chicago	4,127	6,641	Oslo	722	1,162
Colombo	5,854	9,421	Paris	215	346
Copenhagen	609	980	Prague	670	1,078
Djakarta	8,337	13,417	Rome	908	1,461
Geneva	468	753	San Francisco	6,169	9,928
Gibraltar	1,085	1,746	Singapore	7,678	12,357
Hong-Kong	8,102	13,038	Stockholm	899	1,447
Johannesburg	6,227	10,021	Teheran	3,419	5,502
Karachi	4,428	7,126	Tel Aviv	2,230	3,589
Kingston	5,207	8,379	Tokyo	10,066	16,200
Kuala Lumpur	7,883	12,686	Venice	703	1,131
Lagos	3,401	5,473	Vienna	791	1,273
Lisbon	972	1,565	Warsaw	914	1,471
Madrid	775	1,247			

Local Time Throughout the World

As you travel eastwards from Greenwich, the longitude time (see under **Navigation)** is one hour later for every 15°; to the west it is an hour earlier. But for convenience local clocks don't always show the correct longitude time, otherwise travellers inside even a quite small country would be constantly confused. In Britain, all clocks show Greenwich

Mean Time except when Summer Time is in operation. Only in large countries such as Canada, the U.S.S.R., the United States, etc., are time zones necessary.

Summer Time in the United Kingdom is one hour in advance of G.M.T. Many other countries of the world have annual variations from standard time, usually known as Summer Time or Daylight Saving Time. It should be remembered when using the following table, therefore, that there are seasonal variations, and indeed that in the summer local time in Great Britain is 1 p.m. at noon G.M.T.

Here are the local times in various big cities when it is noon (G.M.T.) in London:

City	Time	City	Time
Adelaide		Cape Town	
(Australia)	9.30 p.m.	(South Africa)	2 p.m.
Algiers	1 p.m.	Caracas	
Amsterdam		(Venezuela)	8 a.m.
(Netherlands)	1 p.m.	Chicago (U.S.A.)	6 a.m.
Ankara (Turkey)	2 p.m.	Colombo	
Athens (Greece)	2 p.m.	(Sri Lanka)	5.30 p.m.
Belgrade		Copenhagen	
(Yugoslavia)	1 p.m.	(Denmark)	1 p.m.
Berlin (Germany)	1 p.m.	Djakarta	
Bombay (India)	5.30 p.m.	(Indonesia)	8 p.m.
Boston (U.S.A.)	7 a.m.	Edinburgh	
Brussels (Belgium)	1 p.m.	(Scotland)	noon
Bucharest		Gibraltar	1 p.m.
(Romania)	2 p.m.	Guatemala City	
Budapest		(Guatemala)	6 a.m.
(Hungary)	1 p.m.	Guayaquil	
Buenos Aires		(Ecuador)	7 a.m.
(Argentina)	9 a.m.	Halifax (Canada)	8 a.m.
Cairo (Egypt)	2 p.m.	Havana (Cuba)	7 a.m.
Calcutta (India)	5.30 p.m.	Helsinki (Finland)	2 p.m.
Canton (China)	8 p.m.	Hobart (Tasmania)	10 p.m.

216

Hong Kong	8 p.m.	Peking (China)	8 p.m.
Johannesburg		Perth (Australia)	8 p.m.
(South Africa)	2 p.m.	Prague	
Karachi		(Czechoslovakia)	1 p.m.
(Pakistan)	5 p.m.	Rangoon	
Kingston	7 a.m.	(Burma)	6.30 p.m.
(Jamaica)		Reykjavik	
La Paz (Bolivia)	8 a.m.	(Iceland)	noon
Leningrad		Rio de Janeiro	
(U.S.S.R.)	3 p.m.	(Brazil)	9 a.m.
Lima (Peru)	7 a.m.	Rome (Italy)	1 p.m.
Lisbon (Portugal)	1 p.m.	San Francisco	
Madrid (Spain)	1 p.m.	(U.S.A.)	4 a.m.
Manila (Philippine		Santiago (Chile)	8 a.m.
Islands)	8 p.m.	Shanghai (China)	8 p.m.
Mecca		Singapore	7.30 p.m.
(Saudi Arabia)	3 p.m.	Sofia (Bulgaria)	2 p.m.
Melbourne		Stockholm	
(Australia)	10 p.m.	(Sweden)	1 p.m.
Mexico City		Sydney	
(Mexico)	6 a.m.	(Australia)	10 p.m.
Montevideo		Teheran (Iran)	3.30 p.m.
(Uruguay)	9 a.m.	Tel Aviv (Israel)	2 p.m.
Montreal		Tokyo (Japan)	9 p.m.
(Canada)	7 a.m.	Toronto (Canada)	7 a.m.
Moscow		Vancouver	
(U.S.S.R.)	3 p.m.	(Canada)	4 a.m.
Nairobi (Kenya)	3 p.m.	Vienna (Austria)	1 p.m.
New Orleans		Warsaw (Poland)	1 p.m.
(U.S.A.)	6 a.m.	Wellington	
New York		(New Zealand)	midnight
(U.S.A.)	7 a.m.	Winnipeg	
Oslo (Norway)	1 p.m.	(Canada)	6 a.m.
Panama City		Zürich	
(Panama)	7 a.m.	(Switzerland)	1 p.m.
Paris (France)	1 p.m.		

Great Inventions and Discoveries

Discovery or Invention	Person Responsible	Country	Year
Aeroplane	Wilbur and Orville Wright	United States	1903
Airship	Henri Giffard	France	1852
Atomic Structure	Lord Rutherford	Britain	1910–11
Balloon	Joseph and Jacques Montgolfier	France	1783
Barometer	Evangelista Toricelli	Italy	1643
Bathysphere	W. Bebbe	United States	1934
Bicycle	Kirkpatrick MacMillan	Britain	1839
Clock, Pendulum	Christiaan Huygens	Netherlands	1656
Diesel Engine	Rudolf Diesel	Germany	1897
Dynamite	Alfred Nobel	Sweden	1867
Dynamo	Michael Faraday	Britain	1831
Electric Arc Lamp	Sir Humphry Davy	Britain	1809
Electric Battery	Alessandro Volta	Italy	1800
Electric Lamp, carbon filament	Thomas Edison	United States	1879
Engine, internal combustion (gas)	Etienne Lenoir	France	1860
Engine, internal combustion (petrol)	Gottlieb Daimler	Germany	1883
Engine, Jet	Frank Whittle	Britain	1930
Gas Lighting	William Murdock	Britain	1792
Gramophone	Thomas A. Edison	United States	1877
Gyroscope	Jean Foncault	France	1852
Helicopter	Louis G. Bréguet	France	1909

Hovercraft	C.S. Cockerell	Britain	1955
Lift	Elisha Otis	United States	1852
Lightning Conductor	Benjamin Franklin	United States	1752
Locomotive, Steam	Richard Trevithick	Britain	1801
Machine Gun	Richard Gatling	United States	1862
Match, Friction	John Walker	Britain	1827
Match, Safety	J. E. Lundstrom	Sweden	1855
Microscope, Compound	Zacharias Janssen	Netherlands	1590
Motion-picture Camera	William Friese-Greene	Britain	1888
Motor-car	Karl Benz	Germany	1885
Nylon	W. H. Carothers	United States	1938
Parachute	J. P. Blanchard	France	1785
Penicillin	Sir Alexander Fleming	Britain	1929
Photography	J. Nicéphore Niepce	France	1822
Pianoforte	Bartolommeo Cristofori	Italy	1709
Pneumatic Tyre	Robert Thompson	Britain	1845
Postage Stamp	Sir Rowland Hill	Britain	1840
Power Loom	Edmund Cartwright	Britain	1786
Printing, Movable Type	Johann Gutenberg	Germany	c. 1440
Radar	Robert Watson-Watt	Britain	1935
Radio Telescope	Karl Jansky	United States	1931
Radium	Pierre and Marie Curie	France	1898
Safety Lamp, Miner's	Sir Humphry Davy	Britain	1816
Safety Pin	Walter Hunt	United States	1849
Sewing Machine	Walter Hunt	United States	1832

Sextant	John Hadley	Britain	1731
Steam Engine	James Watt	Britain	1769
Steam Locomotive	Richard Trevithick	Britain	1803
Steam Turbine	Sir Charles A. Parsons	Britain	1884
Stethoscope	René Laennec	France	1816
Tank	Sir Ernest Swinton	Britain	1914
Telephone	Alexander Graham Bell	United States	1876
Telescope, Refracting	Hans Lippershey	Netherlands	1608
Telescope, Reflecting	Isaac Newton	Britain	1669
Television	James Logie Baird	Britain	1926
Torpedo (Modern)	Robert Whitehead	Britain	1868
Transistor	Bardeen, Brattain and Shockley	United States	1948
Typewriter	Christopher Sholes	United States	1868
Umbrella	Samuel Fox	Britain	1852
Vaccination	Edward Jenner	Britain	1796
Wireless Telegraphy	Guglielmo Marconi	Italy	1895
X-rays	Wilhelm Roentgen	Germany	1895

Journeys into Space

We live in the age of man's fastest scientific progress. His curiosity takes him to the Poles, to the deepest parts of the ocean and many miles high into the sky.

What is the sum total so far in the exploration of space—and what may lie ahead within your own lifetime?

The first space probes were the two Russian satellites, *Sputnik I*, and *Sputnik II*, in 1957, which were propelled by multiple-stage rockets to a distance of several hundred miles above the earth's surface, and then directed into orbit so that they circled the earth on a definite course at a speed of about 18,000 miles (29,000 km) per hour.

The Americans launched their first satellites in the early part of 1958, and then, in October, fired a multiple-stage rocket designed to explore the Moon. It was equipped with television gear and it was hoped that it would send back a picture of the far side of the Moon—the side which had never been seen by man.

This was a failure; at some 80,000 feet (24,000m) the flight ended and the object returned to the earth's atmosphere.

In September 1959, the Russian rocket *Lunik II* reached the Moon and photographed its far side.

In August 1960, another Russian rocket was put into orbit containing two dogs. This satellite reached its target back on Earth with the dogs unharmed. In the spring of 1961, the Americans made a similarly successful flight with a chimpanzee.

Then on 12 April of that year came the first man in space, when the Russians sent up Major Yuri Gagarin who made one orbit of the world before landing. This was improved on when fellow-Russian Major Gherman Titov made 17 orbits on August 6, 1961.

Much of America's space prestige was restored when they sent up their first astronaut on February 20, 1962, Colonel John Glenn making three orbits in his *Friendship 7*. This was followed by another three-orbit flight by Major Scott Carpenter in his space capsule *Aurora 7*. Since then, further flights in space have been carried out successfully, unmanned rockets have been fired to the Moon, and information satellites have been launched. In 1965, *Mariner IV* (U.S.A.) sent back to Earth close-up pictures of the surface of Mars, and Major Virgil Grissom (first man to fly twice in space) and Lt. Cdr. John Young completed a two-man American space mission, manoeuvring their craft's height and direction in orbit for the first time. On 15 December, 1965, America's *Gemini VI* and *VII* effected the first-ever human meeting in space. Meanwhile, also in 1965, Col. Belyaev piloted a two-man Russian spaceship while his companion, Lt. Col. Leonov, became the first man to walk into space, floating at the end of a 15 ft. (4·5 m) lifeline for 20 minutes.

In 1967, both American and Russian space probes landed on the Moon and sent information about its surface back to the Earth.

The American space programme reached its climax in July 1969 when the huge *Saturn* V rocket blasted off from Cape Kennedy carrying *Apollo XI* and the three-man crew, Neil Armstrong, Edwin Aldrin and Michael Collins. In the early hours of 21 July, Neil Armstrong became the first human being to set foot on the Moon. He was followed by Aldrin, while Collins piloted the command module orbiting above.

America's 1971 *Apollo 15* mission to the Moon proved an enormous success. That same year the Russians also made a major breakthrough when *Soyuz II* docked with the *Salyut* space station. In 1972 *Mariner 9*, an unmanned spacecraft went into orbit around Mars and sent photographs back to earth that enabled scientists to map 85% of the planet's surface. *Skylab*, an American experimental space station was also launched in this year. 1973–74 saw the longest manned mission to take place in space. From November 16th 1973 to February 8th 1974, the third *Skylab* crew spent a total of 84 days in space, travelling a total distance of 34.5 million miles. In 1975 Russian cosmonauts and American astronauts completed a successful rendezvous when their *Soyuz* and *Apollo* spacecraft docked in space. Two American spacecraft, *Vikings I* and *II*, landed on the surface of Mars, in July and September of 1976. During 1977 NASA successfully carried out space shuttle tests. The shuttle craft was carried to a height of 25,000 feet by a Boeing 747 jet aircraft, and the shuttle craft was flown safely back to earth and landed independently.

PEOPLE AND
THE NEW WORLD

Early American Settlements

It was in the fifteenth century that the people of Europe began to look for new lands in which they could find broader commercial scope and, later, personal freedom. The American continent had been discovered by Scandinavian seamen five centuries earlier, but no settlements had remained. Voyagers such as Christopher Columbus believed that a westward course would lead them to India, and so when they reached America they called it the Indies.

Settlement in North, South and Central America was rapid. The Spanish and Portuguese colonised the South, the French and English the North. The struggles for power lasted for more than a century before the present boundaries and governments became settled. Britain at one time controlled all of eastern North America, but this direct government from London came to an end with the establishment of the United States as an independent nation during the War of 1775-1783 and the creation of Canada as a Dominion in 1867.

The development of the New World has been man's greatest achievement, for it required a mass migration of people, over a long period, from Europe and Africa to colonise such an enormous area as North America, which had previously been inhabited only by wandering indigenous tribes, wrongly called 'Indians'. Two hundred years ago the United States was a group of British colonies on the Eastern seaboard, still struggling to win a living from a new country, to cut back the forests and plough the land in

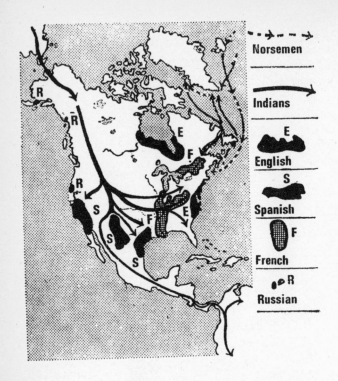

	Norsemen
	Indians
E	English
S	Spanish
F	French
R	Russian

order to grow crops which would pay for their imports from Europe. Today the United States is the wealthiest nation in the world, with one of the highest standards of living. In material assets, it has more cars, telephones, television sets, radios, etc., per thousand of its population than any other nation. Canada, though slower to develop, has raised its standard of living in very much the same way.

Canada

Canada is made up of twelve provinces and territories listed below with their dates of admission as provinces:

Province or Territory	Capital	Date of Admission	Population
Alberta	Edmonton	1905	1,627,874
British Columbia	Victoria	1871	2,184,621
Manitoba	Winnipeg	1870	922,000
New Brunswick	Fredericton	1867	634,577
Newfoundland	St. John's	1949	522,104
Nova Scotia	Halifax	1867	794,000
Ontario	Toronto	1867	7,703,106
Prince Edward Island	Charlottetown	1873	111,641
Quebec	Quebec	1867	6,027,764
Saskatchewan	Regina	1905	926,242
North-West Territories	Ottawa	—	34,807
Yukon Territory	Whitehorse	—	18,388

Ottawa is also the capital of all of Canada.

The United States

The United States is made up of fifty States and the Federal District of Columbia (Washington, D.C.). These are:

Name and Abbreviation	Capital	Date of Admission to the Union
Alabama (Ala.)	Montgomery	1819
Alaska	Juneau	1959
Arizona (Ariz.)	Phoenix	1912
Arkansas (Ark.)	Little Rock	1836
California (Calif.)	Sacramento	1850

Colorado (Colo.)	Denver	1876
Connecticut (Conn.)	Hartford	1788*
Delaware (Del.)	Dover	1787*
District of Columbia (D.C.)	Washington	1791
Florida (Fla.)	Tallahassee	1845
Georgia (Ga.)	Atlanta	1788*
Hawaii	Honolulu	1959
Idaho	Boise	1890
Illinois (Ill.)	Springfield	1818
Indiana (Ind.)	Indianapolis	1816
Iowa (Ia.)	Des Moines	1846
Kansas (Kans.)	Topeka	1861
Kentucky (Ky.)	Frankfort	1792
Louisiana (La.)	Baton Rouge	1812
Maine (Me.)	Augusta	1820
Maryland (Md.)	Annapolis	1788*
Massachusetts (Mass.)	Boston	1788*
Michigan (Mich.)	Lansing	1837
Minnesota (Minn.)	St. Paul	1858
Mississippi (Miss.)	Jackson	1817
Missouri (Mo.)	Jefferson City	1821
Montana (Mont.)	Helena	1889
Nebraska (Nebr.)	Lincoln	1867
Nevada (Nev.)	Carson City	1864
New Hampshire (N.H.)	Concord	1788*
New Jersey (N.J.)	Trenton	1787*
New Mexico (N. Mex.)	Santa Fé	1912
New York (N.Y.)	Albany	1788*
North Carolina (N.C.)	Raleigh	1789*
North Dakota (N. Dak.)	Bismarck	1889
Ohio	Columbus	1803
Oklahoma (Okla.)	Oklahoma City	1907
Oregon (Oreg.)	Salem	1859
Pennsylvania (Pa.)	Harrisburg	1787*
Rhode Island (R.I.)	Providence	1790*
South Carolina (S.C.)	Columbia	1788*

South Dakota (S. Dak.)	Pierre	1889
Tennessee (Tenn.)	Nashville	1796
Texas (Tex.)	Austin	1845
Utah	Salt Lake City	1896
Vermont (Vt.)	Montpelier	1791
Virginia (Va.)	Richmond	1788*
Washington (Wash.)	Olympia	1889
West Virginia (W.Va.)	Charleston	1863
Wisconsin (Wis.)	Madison	1848
Wyoming (Wyo.)	Cheyenne	1890

One of the Thirteen Original States

Growth of the United States in Population

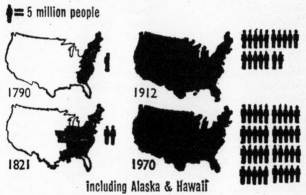

including Alaska & Hawaii

Presidents of the United States

In the American system of government the President combines his Presidential powers with many of those held by a Prime Minister under a system such as that in most Commonwealth countries, and is, therefore, a man of great

227

personal influence during his term of office. The Presidents of the United States have been as follows

George Washington	Federalist	1789
John Adams	Federalist	1797
Thomas Jefferson	Republican	1801
James Madison	Republican	1809
James Monroe	Republican	1817
John Quincy Adams	Republican	1825
Andrew Jackson	Democratic	1829
Martin Van Buren	Democratic	1837
William Henry Harrison	Whig	1841
John Tyler	Whig	1841
James Knox Polk	Democratic	1845
Zachary Taylor	Whig	1849
Millard Fillmore	Whig	1850
Franklin Pierce	Democratic	1853
James Buchanan	Democratic	1857
Abraham Lincoln	Republican	1861
Andrew Johnson	Republican	1865
Ulysses Simpson Grant	Republican	1869
Rutherford Birchard Hayes	Republican	1877
James Abram Garfield	Republican	1881
Chester Alan Arthur	Republican	1881
Grover Cleveland	Democratic	1885 and 1893
Benjamin Harrison	Republican	1889
William McKinley	Republican	1897
Theodore Roosevelt	Republican	1901
William Howard Taft	Republican	1909
Woodrow Wilson	Democratic	1913
Warren Gamaliel Harding	Republican	1921
Calvin Coolidge	Republican	1923
Herbert Clark Hoover	Republican	1929
Franklin Delano Roosevelt	Democratic	1933
Harry S. Truman	Democratic	1945
Dwight D. Eisenhower	Republican	1953
John Fitzgerald Kennedy	Democratic	1961

228

Lyndon B. Johnson	Democratic	1963
Richard M. Nixon	Republican	1969
Gerald R. Ford	Republican	1974
James E. Carter	Democratic	1977

Central and South America and the Caribbean

The countries of Central and South America are independent, with the exception of French Guiana and Surinam (Netherlands Guiana), and a number of island dependencies. They are: —

Name	Date of Gaining Independence
Argentina	1816
Bolivia	1825
Brazil	1822
Chile	1818
Colombia	1819
Costa Rica	1821
Cuba	1902
Dominican Republic	1821
Ecuador	1822
Guatemala	1821
Guyana*	1966
Haiti	1804
Honduras	1821
Jamaica*	1962
Mexico	1810
Nicaragua	1821
Panama	1903
Paraguay	1811
Peru	1821
(El) Salvador	1821
Trinidad and Tobago*	1962
Uruguay	1825
Venezuela	1821

* *Member of the British Commonwealth of Nations*

PEOPLE AND SCIENCE

Weights and Measures

Weights. Imperial System (used in Britain and certain Commonwealth lands, but being replaced gradually by the metric system).

Weights. Metric System

10 milligrammes	=	1 centigramme
10 centigrammes	=	1 decigramme
10 decigrammes	=	1 gramme
10 grammes	=	1 decagramme
10 decagrammes	=	1 hectogramme
10 hectogrammes	=	1 kilogramme
10 kilogrammes	=	1 myriagramme
10 myriagrammes	=	1 quintal
10 quintals	=	1 metric tonne

Weight Conversions

Imperial		Metric	
1 grain	=	0.0648	grammes
1 dram	=	1.772	grammes
1 ounce	=	28.3495	grammes
1 pound	=	0.4536	kilogrammes
1 stone	=	6.35	kilogrammes
1 quarter	=	12.7	kilogrammes
1 hundredweight	=	50.8	kilogrammes
1 ton	=	1,016	kilogrammes
		or 1.016	metric tonnes

Metric		Imperial	
1 milligramme	=	0.015	grains
1 centigramme	=	0.154	grains

1 decigramme	=	1.543 grains
1 gramme	=	15.432 grains
1 decagramme	=	5.644 drams
1 hectogramme	=	3.527 ounces
1 kilogramme	=	2.205 pounds
1 myriagramme	=	22.046 pounds
1 quintal	=	1.968 hundredweights
1 metric tonne	=	0.9842 tons

Measures. Metric System

Linear Measure

10 millimetres	=	1 centimetre
10 centimetres	=	1 decimetre
10 decimetres	=	1 metre
10 metres	=	1 decametre
10 decametres	=	1 hectometre
10 hectometres	=	1 kilometre
10 kilometres	=	1 myriametre

Square Measure

100 square millimetres	=	1 square centimetre
100 square centimetres	=	1 square decimetre
100 square decimetres	=	1 square metre
100 square metres	=	1 are
100 ares	=	1 hectare
100 hectares	=	1 square kilometre

Cubic Measure

1,000 cubic millimetres	=	1 cubic centimetre
1,000 cubic centimetres	=	1 cubic decimetre
1,000 cubic decimetres	=	1 cubic metre

Capacity Measure

10 millilitres	=	1 centilitre
10 centilitres	=	1 decilitre
10 decilitres	=	1 litre
10 litres	=	1 decalitre
10 decalitres	=	1 hectolitre
10 hectolitres	=	1 kilolitre

Measure Conversions

Linear Measure

Imperial   Metric

Imperial		Metric	
1 inch	=	2.54	centimetres
1 foot	=	30.48	centimetres
1 yard	=	0.9144	metres
1 rod	=	5.029	metres
1 chain	=	20.117	metres
1 furlong	=	201.168	metres
1 mile	=	1.6093	kilometres

Metric		Imperial	
1 millimetre	=	0.03937	inches
1 centimetre	=	0.39370	inches
1 decimetre	=	3.93701	inches
1 metre	=	39.3701	inches
		(1.09361	yards)
1 decametre	=	10.9361	yards
1 hectometre	=	109.361	yards
1 kilometre	=	0.62137	miles

Square Measure

Imperial		Metric
1 square inch	=	6.4516 square centimetres
1 square foot	=	9.29 square decimetres
1 square yard	=	0.836 square metres
1 square rod	=	25.293 square metres
1 rood	=	10.117 ares
1 acre	=	0.405 hectares
1 square mile	=	259 hectares

Metric		Imperial
1 square centimetre	=	0.155 square inches
1 square metre	=	10.764 square feet
		(1.196 square yards)
1 are	=	119.6 square yards
1 hectare	=	2.47 acres

Cubic Measure

Imperial		Metric
1 cubic inch	=	16.387 cubic centimetres
1 cubic foot	=	0.0283 cubic metres
1 cubic yard	=	0.7646 cubic metres

Metric		Imperial
1 cubic centimetre	=	0.061 cubic inches
1 cubic decimetre	=	61.024 cubic inches
1 cubic metre	=	35.315 cubic feet
		(1.308 cubic yards)

Capacity Measure

Imperial		Metric	
1 gill	=	1.42	decilitres
1 pint	=	0.568	litres
1 quart	=	1.136	litres
1 gallon	=	4.546	litres
1 bushel	=	36.37	litres
1 quarter	=	2.91	hectolitres

Metric		Imperial	
1 centilitre	=	0.07	gills
1 decilitre	=	0.176	pints
1 litre	=	1.7598	pints
1 decalitre	=	2.2	gallons
1 hectolitre	=	2.75	bushels
		(21.99	gallons)

Nautical Measures

6 feet	=	1 fathom
100 fathoms	=	1 cable
10 cables (6,080 feet)	=	1 nautical mile (1,852 metres)
1 knot	=	1 nautical mile *per hour*

Measure and Sizes for Paper

A0	841 × 1189 mm
A1	594 × 841 mm
A2	420 × 594 mm
A3	297 × 420 mm
A4	210 × 297 mm
RA0	860 × 1220 mm

RA1	610 × 860 mm
RA2	430 × 610 mm
SRA0	900 × 1280 mm
SRA1	640 × 900 mm
SRA2	450 × 640 mm
Metric Quad Crown	768 × 1008 mm
Metric Quad Large Crown	816 × 1056 mm
Metric Quad Demy	888 × 1128 mm
Metric Quad Royal	960 × 1272 mm

Thermometer Readings

The three systems for marking thermometers are Celsius (the Centigrade scale), Fahrenheit and Réaumur. Celsius, which shows 0° for freezing and 100° for boiling water, is used throughout the world for scientific purposes; it is used for general purposes in Europe. Fahrenheit, in which 32° is the freezing temperature and 212° the boiling temperature of water, is the scale previously used in Britain (now transferring to the Centigrade scale) and still employed in the United States. Réaumur, with 0° for freezing and 80° for boiling water, is nearly obsolete, but is occasionally found in old books of European origin on scientific matters and cookery.

A comparison of Celsius and Fahrenheit scales follows:

Celsius		Fahrenheit
—40	=	—40
—30	=	—22
—25	=	—13
—20	=	—4
—17.8	=	0
—15	=	5
—10	=	14
—5	=	23

0	=	32
5	=	41
10	=	50
15	=	59
20	=	68
25	=	77
30	=	86
35	=	95
40	=	104
45	=	113
50	=	122
55	=	131
60	=	140
70	=	158
80	=	176
90	=	194
100	=	212

To change Celsius to Fahrenheit, multiply by 9, divide by 5 and add 32.

To change Fahrenheit to Celsius, subtract 32, multiply by 5 and divide by 9.

Normal blood temperature in human beings is 36.9 °C (98.4 °F).

Roman Numerals

I =	1		IX =	9
II =	2		X =	10
III =	3		XI =	11
IV =	4		XII =	12
V =	5		XIII =	13
VI =	6		XIV =	14
VII =	7		XV =	15
VIII =	8		XVI =	16

XVII =	17		DC =	600
XVIII =	18		DCC =	700
XIX =	19		DCCC =	800
XX =	20		CM =	900
XXX =	30		M =	1,000
XL =	40		MM =	2,000
L =	50		MMM =	3,000
LX =	60		MV̄ =	4,000
LXX =	70		V̄ =	5,000
LXXX =	80		X̄ =	10,000
XC =	90		L̄ =	50,000
C =	100		C̄ =	100,000
CC =	200		D̄ =	500,000
CCC =	300		M̄ =	1,000,000
CD =	400		MCMLXXIV =	1974
D =	500			

Common Formulae

Circumference of Circle	=	$2\pi r$ ($\pi = 3.1416$; r = radius)
Area of Circle	=	πr^2
Volume of Sphere	=	$\frac{4}{3}\pi r^3$
Surface of Sphere	=	$4\pi r^2$
Volume of Cylinder	=	$\pi r^2 h$ (h = height)

Specific Gravity

Glass	=	2.4—2.6
Brass	=	8.1—8.6
Iron	=	8.95
Copper	=	8.95
Silver	=	10.3—10.5
Mercury	=	13.596

Coefficients of Expansion

Glass	=	0.000022
Iron	=	0.000033—0.000044
Copper	=	0.000051
Brass	=	0.000053—0.000057
Gases	=	0.00366

Boiling Points at 760 mm Pressure

Nitrous Oxide	—87.90°C
Chlorine	—33.60°C
Ammonia	—33.50°C
Ether	33.00°C
Chloroform	60.20°C
Alcohol	78.30°C
Benzene	80.40°C
Distilled Water	100.00°C
Sulphuric Acid	325.00°C
Mercury	357.25°C
Sulphur	444.70°C

Speed of Sound

Medium	Feet per Second	Metres per Second
Through Air at 0°C	1,090	332
Through Water	4,758	1.450

Through Carbon Dioxide	850	259
Through Hydrogen	4,160	1.268
Through Glass	approx. 16,500	5.030

Chemical Names of Everyday Substances

Substance	Chemical Name
Alcohol	Ethyl Alcohol
Alum	Aluminium Potassium Sulphate
Baking Powder	Sodium Bicarbonate
Boracic Acid	Boric Acid
Borax	Sodium Borate
Chalk	Calcium Carbonate
Common Salt	Sodium Chloride
Epsom Salts	Magnesium Sulphate
Fire-damp	Methane
Glauber Salts	Sodium Sulphate
Hypo	Sodium Thiosulphate
Lime	Calcium Oxide
Magnesia	Magnesium Oxide
Plaster of Paris	Calcium Sulphate
Red Lead	Triplumbic Tetroxide
Sal Ammoniac	Ammonium Chloride
Saltpetre	Potassium Nitrate
Salts of Lemon	Potassium Hydrogen Oxalate
Sal Volatile	Ammonium Carbonate
Spirits of Salts	Hydrochloric Acid
Vinegar	Dilute Acetic Acid
Washing Soda	Crystalline Sodium Carbonate
White Lead	Basic Lead Carbonate

Chemical Indicators

Indicators show whether a substance is alkaline, acid or neutral. The following list gives the effect of adding an indicator.

Indicator	Alkaline	Acid	Neutral
Litmus	turns blue	turns red	turns purple
Methyl Orange	turns yellow	turns pink	remains orange

Wind Force

When weather forecasters want to inform ships of the exact strength of winds likely to blow in their areas, they do so by using the Beaufort Scale, referring to 'Force 2' or 'Force 5', or whatever is appropriate. The Scale is given overleaf...

Force Number	Description	M.P.H.
0	Calm	0 — 1
1	Light air	1 — 3
2	Light breeze	4 — 7
3	Gentle breeze	8 — 12
4	Moderate breeze	13 — 18
5	Fresh breeze	19 — 24
6	Strong breeze	25 — 31
7	Near gale	32 — 38
8	Gale	39 — 46
9	Strong gale	47 — 54
10	Storm	55 — 63
11	Violent storm	64 — 73
12	Hurricane	over 73

PEOPLE AND LANGUAGE

The Development of the Alphabet. We do not know the point in man's development at which he first made sound which could be described as 'language'. The tracing of the history of written language, however, has been possible to a high degree of accuracy, and the diagram on the following page indicates how most of our present-day letters came to be formed.

Column I shows Egyptian hieroglyphics, or picture-writing, facing to the left. Column II is of later Egyptian writing, in which the picture has become unrecognisable, and the direction has changed to the right. Column III shows the progress made by the time of the Phoenicians and Column VI contains the fairly similar alphabet of early Greek civilisation. Columns V, VI and VII show further development by the Greeks; in Columns VIII, IX and X are the stages through which the Romans progressed, leaving as their legacy most of the present-day alphabet of the Western world.

The English Language

Our own language, English, is a mixture of words drawn from the vocabularies of the various invaders of Britain over a period of some two thousand years. That is why in English there are often several different words meaning roughly the same thing, some having Anglo-Saxon origins and others coming from Latin. Our language is also less 'regular' than French, Italian or Spanish, all of which have direct Latin origins.

Words are placed in categories according to how they are used. These categories are known as parts of speech. The English language has eight parts of speech. They are listed below.

Noun : the name of a person, place or thing. Nouns are of four Genders: Masculine, Feminine, Common and Neuter.

241

	EGYPTIAN			GREEK				LATIN		
1				A	A		a	A	A	aaa
2				B	B	B	B	B	B	Bb
3				1	Γ	Γ		<	C	c
4				Δ	Δ		δ	D	D	dd
5					E	E	ε	E	E	ee
6				Y	VF		F	F	F	Ff
7				I	I	Z		Z	Z	z
8				Θ	H	H		Θ	H	hh
9				⊕	⊙	Θ		⊕		
10					I	I		I	I	ij
11					K	K	KK	K	K	k
12					Λ	λ		L	L	ll
13				M	M	M			M	mm
14					N	N			N	nn
15					Ξ					xx
16				o	O	O	o	O		
17					Γ	π		P	P	P
18				M	M					
19				φ	φ			φ	Q	qq
20					P	P		R	R	
21						C		S	S	fs
22				T	T	T		T	T	t

These Genders can be illustrated by the following words: man, woman, cousin, hat. Nouns are either Singular or Plural, examples of both being: dog and dogs, penny and pence. Classes of nouns are Proper (the name of a particular person, place or thing, e.g. William, France) and Common (the name common to everything in one group, e.g. house, car).

English nouns have three Cases which they take to show their relation to the rest of a sentence. These are Nominative (denoting the person or thing taking action), Objective (the person or thing about which action is taken) and Possessive (that which belongs to a person or thing).

Adjective: a word which describes or qualifies a noun. Adjectives may be divided into three categories: those which express Quality (*bad* company), those expressing Quantity (*ten* boys) and Demonstrative Adjectives (*that* window). There are three degrees of comparison in adjectives—Positive, Comparative and Superlative, examples of which are: good, better, best; young, younger, youngest.

The Articles (Definite: the; Indefinite: a, an) are also adjectives, as are the Numerals (Cardinal: one, two; Ordinal: first, second; Multiplicative: once, twice; Indefinite: many, few).

Pronoun: a word used in place of a noun. Pronouns, like nouns, have Gender, Number and Case. Pronouns may be Personal (I, she, you), Relative (that, who), Demonstrative (this, those), Indefinite (some, one), Interrogative (who? which?), Distributive (either, each) and Reflexive (yourself, themselves).

Verb: a word which states the action of a noun. Verbs are either Transitive or Intransitive. Transitive verbs describe an action which affects an object, e.g. 'I start the car'. Intransitive verbs do not affect an object, e.g. 'The car starts.' 'I start the car' is an example of a verb in Active Voice; in Passive Voice it would be 'The car was started by me.'

243

Verbs have three Finite Moods: Indicative (I speak); Imperative (Speak!); Subjunctive (I may speak). There is also the Infinitive Mood (to speak).

There are two Participles, used with such verbs as *to be* and *to have*: the Present Participle (speaking) and the Past Participle (spoken). There is also a verbal noun, the Gerund (the *speaking* of English).

The Tense of a verb shows the time of its action (Past, Present, Future). The degrees of completeness of the action are: Simple (I speak, I spoke, I shall speak); Continuous (I am speaking; I was speaking, I shall be speaking); Perfect (I have spoken, I had spoken, I shall have spoken); Perfect Continuous (I have been speaking, I had been speaking I shall have been speaking).

Adverb: a word which modifies or qualifies a verb, an adjective or another adverb. Adverbs can be divided into the following categories: Time (often, now); Place (here, outside); Quality (well, beautifully); Quantity (enough, almost); Number (once); Cause (therefore, why); Mood (perhaps).

Preposition: a word which shows the relation between words in a sentence. Examples of prepositions are: to, on, by, of, from, for, through, about, after, except, towards.

Conjunction: a word which links words, phrases, clauses or sentences. Examples of conjunctions are: and, but, for, because, also, unless, though, therefore.

Interjection: a word standing alone in a sentence, expressing strong emotion. Examples are: Indeed! Goodness! Bother! Oh! Alas!

Foreign Words and Phrases

There are many foreign expressions used in English, a number of which are quite convenient in that there is no exact equivalent in our language. Here are some in common use (Abbreviations—F: French; G: German; Gk: Greek; I: Italian; L: Latin; P: Portuguese; S: Spanish).

244

ad hoc (L). For this special object.
ad infinitum (L). For ever; to infinity.
ad interim (L). Meanwhile.
ad libitum (ad lib.) (L). To any extent; at pleasure.
ad nauseam (L). To the point of disgust.
adsum (L). I am here.
ad valorem (L). According to value.
affaire d'honneur (F). Affair of honour; duel.
a fortiori (L). With stronger reason.
à la bonne heure (F). Well done; that's good.
à la carte (F). From the full menu.
à la mode (F). In the fashion.
alter ego (L). Other self.
amour-propre (F). Self-esteem.
a posteriori (L). From the effect to the cause.
a priori (L). From the cause to the effect.
à propos (F). To the point.
arrière-pensée (F). Mental reservation.
au contraire (F). On the contrary.
au courant (F). Fully acquainted (with).
auf Wiedersehen (G). Till we meet again.
au naturel (F). In a natural state.
au pair (F). On an exchange basis.
au revoir (F). Till we meet again.
auto da fé (P). Act of faith.
à votre santé (F). Your good health!

bête noire (F). Pet hate.
billet doux (F). Love letter.
bona fide (L). In good faith; genuine.
bon marché (F). A bargain; cheap.
bon vivant (F). Gourmet; one who enjoys life.
bon voyage (F). Have a good journey.

canaille (F). Common mob (term of contempt).
carpe diem (L). Enjoy today.

carte blanche (F). Full powers.

casus belli (L). Cause of war.

caveat emport (L). Let the buyer beware.

chacun à son goût (F). Everyone to his own taste.

chef-d'oeuvre (F). Masterpiece.

cherchez la femme (F). Look for the woman (in the case).

ci-devant (F). Former.

comme il faut (F). In good taste.

compos mentis (L). In full possession of sanity.

corps de ballet (F). The team of dancers in a ballet.

corps diplomatique (F). The group of diplomats in a capital city.

cui bono? (L). Who will get any benefit?

cum grano salis (L). With a grain of salt.

d'accord (F). Agreed.

de facto (L). In fact.

de jure (L). By right (in law).

de luxe (F). Of especially high quality.

de rigueur (F). Necessary.

dernier cri (F). The latest fashion.

de trop (F). Superfluous; not wanted.

deus ex machina (L). Providential interposition; nick-of-time solution by a superhuman agency.

Dieu et mon droit (F). God and my right (motto of the British Crown).

double entente (F). Double meaning (sometimes *double entendre*).

embarras de richesse (F). Difficulty caused by having too much.

en deshabillé (F). Dressed in clothes suitable only for lounging.

en famille (F). In the family; informal.

en fête (F). Clebrating.

en passant (F). In passing; by the way.

246

en rapport (F). In sympathy; in harmony.
entre nous (F). Between ourselves.
esprit de corps (F). Group spirit.
ex cathedra (L). From the chair of office, with authority.
ex libris (L). From the books (of).

fait accompli (F). An accomplished fact.
faux pas (F). False step; mistake.
femme de chambre (F). Chambermaid.
fête champêtre (F.) Gala occasion in the open air.
fiat lux (L). Let there be light.
fin de siècle (F). Decadent.

gitano (S). Gipsy.
gourmet (F). Lover of good food.

Hausfrau (G). Housewife.
hic jacet (L). Here lies.
hoi poliol (Gk). The people.
honi soit qui mal y pense (F). Shamed be he who thinks evil of it.
hors de combat (F). No longer able to fight.

ibidem (ibid.) (L). In the same place.
ich dien (G). I serve.
idée fixe (F). Obsession.
in extremis (L). At the point of death.
infra dignitatem (infra dig.) (L). Beneath one's dignity.
in loco parentis (L). In the place of a parent.
in memoriam (L). In memory (of).
in perpetuum (L). For ever.
in re (L). In the matter of.
in situ (L). In its original position.
inter alia (L). Among other things.
in toto (L). Completely.
ipso facto (L). (Obvious) from the facts.
ipso jure (L). By the law itself.

je ne sais quoi (F). I know not what.
jeu d'esprit (F). Witticism.

laissez faire (F). Leave matters alone: a policy of non-interference.
lares et penates (L). Household gods.
lèse-majesté (F). High treason or arrogant conduct of inferiors.
locum tenens (L). A substitute or deputy.

magnum opus (L). A great work; an author's principal book.
maitre d'hôtel (F). Hotel-keeper; head waiter.
mal de mer (F). Sea-sickness.
mañana (S). Tomorrow (will do as well as today).
mariage de convenance (F). A marriage arranged for money or other material considerations.
mea culpa (L). It is my fault.
modus operandi (L). Method of working.
multum in parvo (L). Much in little.
mutatis mutandis (L). The necessary changes having been made.

non plus ultra (L). Nothing further; the summit of achievement.
nil desperandum (L). Despair of nothing.
noblesse oblige (F). Noble birth imposes obligations.
nom de guerre (F). Assumed name.
nom de plume (F). Assumed name of an author.
non compos mentis (L). Of unsound mind.
non sequitur (L). It does not follow.
nota bene (N. B.) (L). Note well.
nouveau riche (F). Newly rich.

opus (L). Work (of art, music or literature).

248·

outré (F). Eccentric; outside the bounds of propriety.

pace (L). By leave of.
par excellence (F). Pre-eminently.
par exemple (F). For example.
passim (L). Everywhere.
pax vobiscum (L). Peace be with you.
per annum (L). By the year.
per capita (L). By the head.
per centum (per cent) (L). By the hundred.
per diem (L). By the day.
per mensem (L). By the month.
persona grata (L). An acceptable person.
persona non grata (L). An unacceptable person.
pièce de résistance (F). Chief dish of meal; main item.
pied-à-terre (F). Lodging for occasional visits.
poste restante (F). To await collection (from a post office).
prima ballerina (I). Principal female dancer in a ballet.
prima donna (I). Principal female singer in an opera.
prima facie (L). At first sight.
pro forma (L). As a matter of form.
pro rata (L). In proportion.
prosit (G). Good health!
pro tempore (L). For the time being.

quid pro quo (L). Something offered for another of the same value.
quien sabe? (S). Who knows?
quo vadis (L). Whither thou goest?

raison d'être (F). Reason for existence.
rara avis (L). A rare bird; unusual person or thing.
reduction ad absurdum (L). A reducing to the absurd.
rendez-vous (F). Meeting-place.
requiescat in pace (R. I. P.) (L). Rest in peace.
résumé (F). Summary.

sans souçi (F). Without care.
sauve qui peut (F). Save himself who can.
savoir-faire (F). Tact.
semper fidelis (L). Always faithful.
sine die (L). Indefinitely.
sine qua non (L). An indispensable condition.
sobriquet (F). Nickname.
soi-disant (F). Self-styled.
sotto voce (I). In a whisper or undertone.
status quo (L). The existing state of affairs.
stet (L). Let it stand (ignore correction marks).
sub judice (L). Before a judge (and not yet decided).
sub rosa (L). Under the rose; secretly.
sui generis (L). Of its own kind; unique.

table d'hôte (F). A set meal at a fixed price.
tempus fugit (L). Time flies.
terra firma (L). Solid earth.
tête-à-tête (F). Private talk between two people.
tour de force (F). Feat of skill or strength.
tout de suite (F). Immediately.
tout ensemble (F). Taken all together.

ubique (L). Everywhere.
ultima Thule (L). The utmost boundary.

vade mecum (L). A constant companion; a manual of reference.
versus (L). Against.
vice versa (L). Conversely.
vis-à-vis (F). Opposite; face to face.

wagon-lit (F). Railway sleeping-car.
Weltschmerz (G). World weariness.

Zeitgeist (G). Spirit of the times.

Boys Names

Here are the meanings and derivations of some of the more common boy's names. Diminutives have not been included— for example Eddie, Ned and Teddy are not listed as they have the same meaning as Edward.

Adam (Hebrew): "man of earth."
Adrian (Latin): "man of the seacoast."
Alan (Celtic): "harmony, cheerful."
Albert (Teutonic): "noble and bright."
Alexander (Greek): "protector of men."
Alfred (Anglo-Saxon): "wise as an elf, counsellor."
Andrew (Greek): "manly."
Anthony (Latin): "worthy; strong."
Arthur (Celtic): "strong as a rock."
Bernard (Teutonic): "grim bear."
Brian (Celtic): "strong; powerful."
Charles (Teutonic): "man."
Christopher (Greek): "Christ-bearer."
Colin (Celtic): "dove."
Craig (Celtic): "of the crag or stony hill."
Cyril (Greek): "Lord."
Daniel (Hebrew): "the Lord is judge."
David (Hebrew): "beloved."
Dennis (Greek): "lover of fine wines."
Derek (Teutonic): "the people's ruler."
Desmond (Celtic): "worldly; sophisticated."
Donald (Celtic): "proud chief."
Douglas (Celtic): "dark grey; from the dark stream."
Edgar (Angle-Saxon): "lucky spear; fortunate warrior."
Edmund (Anglo-Saxon): "fortunate or rich protector."
Edward (Anglo-Saxon): "prosperous guardian."
Eric (Teutonic): "kingly."
Ernest (Teutonic): "sincere; earnest."
Francis (Teutonic): "free."

Frederick (Teutonic): "peaceful ruler."
Gary (Anglo-Saxon): "mighty spear."
Geoffrey (Teutonic): "God's peace; peace of the land."
George (Greek): "farmer; tiller of the soil."
Gerald (Teutonic): "firm spearman."
Gilbert (Teutonic): "bright pledge."
Gordon (Anglo-Saxon): "from the cornered hill."
Graham (Teutonic): "from the grey home."
Gregory (Greek): "vigilant."
Guy (French): "guide; leader."
Harold (Anglo-Saxon): "powerful warrior."
Henry (Teutonic): "home ruler."
Herbert (Teutonic): "bright warrior."
James (Hebrew): "the supplanter."
Jeremy (Hebrew): "exalted by the Lord."
John (Hebrew): "God's gracious gift."
Joseph (Hebrew): "He shall add."
Keith (Celtic): "a place."
Kenneth (Celtic): "handsome."
Kevin (Celtic): "kind; gentle."
Lawrence (Latin): "laurel; crowned with laurel."
Leonard (Latin): "lion; brave as a lion."
Leslie (Celtic): "from the grey fort."
Louis, Lewis (Teutonic): "renowned in battle."
Malcolm (Celtic): "servant."
Mark, Martin (Latin): "belonging to Mars; a warrior."
Matthew (Hebrew): "God's gift."
Maurice (Latin): "dark; Moorish."
Michael (Hebrew): "Godlike."
Neville (Latin): "from the new town."
Nicholas (Greek): "victory of the people."
Nigel (Latin): "dark; black."
Noel (Latin): "Christmas."
Oliver (Latin): "olive; peace."
Patrick (Latin): "noble; patrician."
Paul (Latin): "small."

252

Peter (Greek): "rock."
Philip (Greek): "lover of horses."
Raymond (Teutonic): "wise protection."
Reginald (Teutonic): "powerful judgement."
Richard (Teutonic): "powerful king."
Robert (Teutonic): "of shining fame."
Rodney (Teutonic): "renowned."
Roland (Teutonic): "fame of the land."
Rudolph (Teutonic): "famed wolf."
Samuel (Hebrew): "asked of God."
Simon (Hebrew): "hearer."
Stephen (Greek): "crowned."
Stewart (Anglo-Saxon): "keeper of the estate."
Terence (Latin): "tender."
Thomas (Hebrew): "a twin."
Timothy (Greek): "honouring God."
Vernon (Latin): "growing green; flourishing."
Victor (Latin): "the conqueror."
Vincent (Latin): "the conqueror."
William (Teutonic): "helmet of resolution."

Girls Names

Abigail (Hebrew) "Father rejoiced."
Alexandra (Russian) from the Greek Alexander "Defending men."
Alice (Old French). Alison is the Scottish form.
Amelia (German) "struggling, labour."
Amy (Old French) from the verb aimer, "to love."
Ann, Anne, Anna, from the Hebrew Hannah meaning "God has favoured me."
Anthea (Greek) "flowery."
Annabel, from Ämabel (Latin) "lovable."
Beatrice, Beatrix (Latin) "Bringer of joy."
Brenda, a Shetland name from the Norse "brand" meaning "sword."

253

Bridget (Celt) "strength."
Candida (Latin) "white."
Carol, Caroline, feminine forms of Charles.
Catherine, Katharine, Katrine, Kathleen (Latin) "pure."
Celia, from Roman name meaning "heavenly."
Chloe (Greek) "a green shoot."
Christian, Christine (Latin) "belonging to Christ."
Clara, Clarissa (Latin) "bright."
Cordelia (Latin) "warm hearted."
Daisy (English) a Victorian name from the French Marguerite meaning daisy.
Daphne (Greek) "laurel."
Deborah (Hebrew) "bee."
Deirdre (Irish) "doubtful."
Denise (French) from the Greek Dionysius God of Wine.
Delores (Spanish) "sorrows."
Diana (Latin) "goddess."
Dulcie (Latin) "sweet."
Edith (Old Eng) "happy."
Eileen (Irish) "pleasant."
Elaine (Old French) a form of Helen.
Eleanor, Leonora, Ella, Ellen – all from Helen.
Elizabeth, Elisabeth (Hebrew) "an oath."
Elspeth, Scottish form of Elizabeth.
Esmerelda (Spanish) "emerald."
Eva (Hebrew) "life."
Fiona (Gaelic) "fair."
Flora (Latin) name of the Roman flower goddess.
Florence (Latin) "blooming."
Frances, form of Francis (Latin) meaning "a Frenchman."
Genevieve (French) "Obscure."
Gill, Gillian, from Juliana (Latin) "belonging to Julius."
Grace (French) "grace."
Gwendolyn (Welsh) "white."
Hannah, see Ann.

254

Hazel, Heather, both English names which become popular early 1900's, after the flower and tree of the same name.

Helen (Greek) meaning "the bright one."

Henrietta, feminine form of Henry (Latin) introduced from France.

Hilary (Latin) from Hilarius meaning "cheerful."

Honor, (Anglo-Norman) from Latin meaning "reputation" and "beauty."

Imogen, Imogine (Old English) possibly based on the Greek word for grand-daughter.

Ingrid (Norwegian).

Irene (Greek) from Eirene, the Greek goddess of "peace."

Isobel, Isabella (Latin) used in France and Spain as the equivalent of Elizabeth.

Jacqueline (French) the feminine form of Jacques (James).

Jane (Old French) originally from Jehane. Earlier usage was Joanna. Pet names Janey and Jenny.

Janet, a Scottish variation of Jane.

Jennifer, from Guenevere (Welsh) the name of the wife of King Arthur.

Jemima (Hebrew) "dove."

Joan, feminine form of John, also from Old French name Jehane.

Judith (Hebrew) meaning "Jewess."

Juliet, Julia, taken from the Italian name Giulia and used by Shakespeare.

Katherine, see Catherine.

Karen, the Danish form of Katherine.

Kirsty (Scottish) form of Christian and Christine.

Laura (Latin) from the word for laurel tree.

Louise (French) the feminine form of Louis.

Lynn (Celtic) "a lake."

Margaret, from (Greek) meaning "a pearl."

Mary (English) from the Hebrew Maraim which means "to be fat."

Marie, Maria, both derived from the same as Mary.

Melanie, from the Greek word meaning "black" or "dark complexioned."

Miranda (Latin) "worthy of admiration."

Nancy, from Anne.

Naomi (Hebrew) "pleasant one."

Natalie, from the Latin Natalis, commonly used in France and Germany, and in Russia as the name Natasha.

Olivia (Italian) English form is Olive.

Ophelia, probably from Greek, meaning "help", and "succour."

Patricia, the feminine form of Patrick.

Penelope (Greek) "a weaver."

Phillipa, the English feminine form of Philip.

Polly, a pet form of Mary, just as Molly is.

Rachel (Hebrew) "a ewe", signifying gentleness.

Rebecca (Hebrew) "a snare."

Rhoda (Greek) "roses or rose-bush."

Rosalind, from the Latin meaning "fair as a rose."

Sara, Sarah (Hebrew) "the princess."

Sophie, Sophia (Greek) "wisdom."

Susanna(h) (Hebrew) "graceful white lily." Susan, Sue, Susie are all pet forms of this name.

Teresa, originally from the Greek meaning "a reaper." Pet forms Tess and Tessa.

Tina, from Christina.

Truda, from Gertrude.

Trixy, from Beatrix.

Una (Irish) probably based on the word for "lamb."

Ursula (Latin) "little she bear."

Vanessa, Van in Hebrew means "Grace of God."

Victoria, from Latin for "victory."

Vivien (Latin) "alive."

Wendy (Teutonic) "the wanderer."

Winifrid, (Celtic) "white wave or stream."

Yvonne (French) feminine form of Yves.

Zoe (Greek) "life."

256